Inclusive Classroom Profile (ICP™) Manual, Research Edition

D1597269

Inclusive Classroom Profile (ICP™) Manual, Research Edition

by

Elena P. Soukakou, D.Phil.
Roehampton University

·P·A·U·L·H·
BROOKES
PUBLISHING CO ®

Baltimore • London • Sydney

Paul H. Brookes Publishing Co.
Post Office Box 10624
Baltimore, Maryland 21285-0624
USA

www.brookespublishing.com

"Paul H. Brookes Publishing Co." is a registered trademark
of Paul H. Brookes Publishing Co., Inc.

"ICP™" and **ICP** are trademarks of Paul H. Brookes
Publishing Co., Inc.

Typeset by Absolute Services, Baltimore, Maryland.
Manufactured in the United States of America by
Sheridan Books, Chelsea, Michigan.

All examples in this book are composites. Any similarity to
actual individuals or circumstances is coincidental, and no
implications should be inferred.

This manual accompanies the Inclusive Classroom Profile (ICP™),
Research Edition. To order, contact Paul H. Brookes Publishing Co.
(1-800-638-3775; 410-337-9580; www.brookespublishing.com).

Library of Congress Cataloging-in-Publication Data

The Library of Congress has cataloged the printed edition as follows:

Names: Soukakou, Elena P., 1976- author.
Title: The Inclusive Classroom Profile (ICP™) Manual / Elena P. Soukakou, D.Phil.,
    Roehampton University.
Description: Research edition. | Baltimore, Maryland: Brookes Publishing,
    2016. | Includes bibliographical references and index.
Identifiers: LCCN 2016028913 | ISBN 9781598579918 (paperback)
Subjects: LCSH: Inclusive education--Evaluation--Handbooks, manuals, etc. |
    Children with disabilities--Education (Early childhood)--Handbooks,
    manuals, etc. | BISAC: EDUCATION / Special Education / General. |
    EDUCATION / Special Education / Mental Disabilities. | EDUCATION /
    Professional Development.
Classification: LCC LC1200 .S68 2016 | DDC 371.9/046--dc23 LC record
    available at https://lccn.loc.gov/2016028913

British Library Cataloguing in Publication data are available from the British Library.

2025   2024   2023   2022   2021

10   9   8   7   6   5   4   3

Contents

About the Author

Elena P. Soukakou, D.Phil., is Senior Lecturer in the School of Education at Roehampton University, United Kingdom. Dr. Soukakou earned her doctoral degree in education from Oxford University, United Kingdom. She began her career as an early childhood special education teacher upon graduating from Teachers College, Columbia University. She has worked for more than 10 years as an early intervention specialist, researcher, and consultant for early childhood inclusion and special education in the United States, United Kingdom, and her home country, Greece.

She received the Distinguished Early Career Award of the Early Education and Child Development Special Interest Group of the American Educational Research Association (AERA) in 2013 for her work on the Inclusive Classroom Profile. Dr. Soukakou works collaboratively with early childhood educators, professionals, researchers, and leaders in the field to support the inclusion of young children with disabilities and their families in all aspects of early childhood education and care.

Foreword

In *Inclusive Classroom Profile (ICP™), Research Edition,* Elena P. Soukakou gives early childhood education a long-awaited assessment tool that can truly move our work in early childhood inclusive practice forward. Carefully designed, the ICP looks closely at the ways inclusive programs accommodate the learning needs of young children with disabilities and provides not only a measure of program quality but also a framework for program planning and professional development. The ICP reflects Dr. Soukakou's extensive study of inclusive preschool classrooms both in the United Kingdom and the United States and her deep understanding of what is needed to provide optimal access and full participation in the curriculum for all children. The ICP articulates the importance of environmental support for all learners and clarifies distinctions between multiple levels of quality practice.

With a design that is easily accessible to program evaluators, teachers, and researchers, the ICP can be used to assess program quality with a single classroom observation and brief teacher interview. The items measured give insight into both the physical and interpersonal environments provided within inclusive classrooms, allowing teachers and administrators to see areas of a program's success or determine where improvement is needed. This tool can also be used for research on inclusive classrooms, providing clear comparisons between quality practices within different programs and measurements of the degree to which children's needs are being met. Additionally, information gathered from the ICP can provide guidelines for programs and faculty that are striving to enact optimal inclusive teaching and learning experiences for the children they serve.

An exceptionally useful and well-developed assessment, the ICP is carefully designed, extensively field tested, and thoughtfully refined to capture the quality of day-to-day inclusive classroom experiences for young children with disabilities. Each of the 12 items included in the ICP is in line with research-based knowledge on effective inclusive teaching. The capacities reflected in these items are broad enough to be applied to a wide range of early childhood programs and settings serving children with diverse needs. The ICP's scoring system allows the user to identify qualitative differences in daily inclusive practices.

In recent years, early childhood scholars developed a strong philosophical stance toward inclusion along with numerous guidelines for inclusive teaching. The ICP takes us one step further by providing a system for clearly seeing how teaching and learning are actually occurring within inclusive classrooms. It adds depth and complexity to current understandings of quality in early childhood programs by articulating components of daily practice that contribute substantively to young children's experiences of inclusion. Elements of practice included in the ICP do more than serve as a tool for assessing quality environments. They also provide a framework for creating early childhood classrooms that nurture active participation and a sense of community for all children learning together.

The ICP offers a value-added component to existing program quality measures, which fail to look closely at the ways that programs support children with disabilities or special learning needs. I look forward to sharing the ICP with my students and colleagues and see great potential for this assessment to inform and support quality early childhood inclusive practice.

Susan L. Recchia, Ph.D.
Professor and Coordinator
Programs in Early Childhood and Early Childhood Special Education
Teachers College, Columba University
Coauthor, Inclusion in the Early Childhood Classroom: What Makes a Difference?

It is an honor and a pleasure to contribute a foreword to the *Inclusive Classroom Profile (ICP™) Manual, Research Edition,* an innovative addition to the rapidly growing suite of observational tools for assessing quality in early childhood settings. The ICP has many strengths: it has sound psychometric properties that have been established in the United States and in England, two countries with different approaches to the inclusion of children with special educational needs and/or disabilities. Its strong validity in both countries demonstrates the wide applicability of the scale's underlying constructs of inclusion. Next, the very helpful guidance notes and rigorous training program will equip professionals with the skills they need to produce objective assessments for use in research, professional development, and accreditation. Finally, the ICP focuses on pedagogy and resources that will foster learning in children with additional needs, and as important, their inclusion in peer groups and the classroom community. Some of its most innovative items judge the quality of practices employed by staff to ensure rich social engagement *for all children*, such as "encouraging other peers to support children who find it difficult to engage in social interactions" (p. 15).

This assessment is an outstanding example of the many new means for implementing evidence-based practice in early childhood settings. I first encountered the ICP in the original sample of 45 English preschools, all exemplars of inclusive practice within the English Early Years Foundation Stage curriculum. Not only did the ICP have impressive standards of inter-observer reliability, but it also was validated against other quality measures such as the The Early Childhood Environment Rating Scale-Revised (ECERS-R) and the Early Childhood Environment Rating Scale-Extension (ECERS-E). Findings from the initial validation study (Soukakou, 2012) showed that it was possible for a setting to receive high scores on global quality (whole classroom) but offer lower quality to the children included by reason of special needs or disability. This convinced me of the urgent need for a separate scale, one focused on the specifics of inclusive practices or resources that research has shown to be beneficial for children with additional needs.

After its origin in English practice, the scale was further developed in the U.S. context and extensive trialling was carried out (Soukakou, Winton, West, Sideris, & Rucker, 2015). A rigorous training program was developed, along with more extensive guidance notes and further research on validity. The scales that follow have had the benefit of wide consultation with a range of professionals including researchers, trainers, classroom staff, and managers.

The ICP follows the seven–point-scale format of the Early Childhood Rating Scales (ERS), therefore, it can easily supplement these global instruments with a sharp focus on provision for those with additional needs. Great strides have been made in inclusive practice, but there remains a need to document and assess process quality in systematic and transparent ways. Use of the ICP will be a powerful means to document effective practice and guide settings in quality improvement. This observational tool has taken more than a decade in development. Its slow gestation has allowed careful field-test, wide consultation, and rigorous research–the hallmarks of today's evidence-based practice.

Kathy Sylva, Ph.D.
Professor
University of Oxford

Preface

The Inclusive Classroom Profile (ICP™) started as a doctoral research project at Oxford University in the United Kingdom (2003–2008). At the time, I was reviewing the literature on teaching practices and interventions implemented in early childhood inclusive programs. By inclusive programs I mean early childhood education settings in which children with identified disabilities participate alongside their peers without disabilities. The questions I was asking at the time included, "What classroom practices and instructional supports can best meet the needs of young children with identified disabilities in early childhood programs?" "What practices can support children's individual learning needs while they also encourage children's active participation and membership in the classroom's life?" "How can practitioners responsible for educating young children with special education needs be supported so that they can implement high-quality inclusive practices in their classrooms?" Although the ICP was originally designed in the United Kingdom, its development was guided by international research on preschool inclusion. The ICP has undergone many revisions since its initial conception, and it has been piloted and used in several research studies and demonstration projects in the United States, United Kingdom, and other countries (Portugal, Turkey, Sweden, and Greece) since the mid-2000s.

As a trained special education teacher and having worked in many different types of inclusive programs in the United States and the United Kingdom, I recognize the importance of selecting and implementing individually appropriate and effective practices to meet the diverse needs of children in early childhood settings. I was exposed to a wide range of teaching approaches and interventions across my own practice as a teacher and consultant. Still, however, the day-to-day application of these within the context of daily classroom interactions and children's diverse learning profiles proved far more complex. Deciding which practices and interventions would be most suitable for the children within my classroom was my first challenge. Another challenge related to the process of individualizing instructional supports for a particular child or group of children in the classroom while at the same time encouraging participation in the daily classroom activities with their peers. I have learned through my collaborative work with early childhood teachers and other practitioners that teachers often face similar challenges in their everyday practice.

Practicing high-quality inclusion can be particularly challenging in the absence of valid and reliable tools that can guide early childhood educators, special education teachers, and specialist teams to identify and assess the quality of their implemented practices. Although current early childhood environment measures and formative assessment tools of classroom quality are useful in capturing the quality of the physical environment and teaching approaches implemented with most preschool children, they are not often designed to focus on the strategies that might be necessary for meeting the needs of children with disabilities included in early childhood classrooms.

From this perspective, the ICP was designed to be used by early childhood educators, assessors, professional development providers, special education teachers, and researchers as a resource of inclusive practices that have a strong evidence base and are recommended in the field of early childhood special education for supporting high-quality inclusion. As a quality assessment and improvement tool, my hope is that the ICP will support users in reflecting on important dimensions of inclusive practice, identifying areas for improvement, and developing relevant action plans to support the diverse learning and developmental needs of children included in early childhood classrooms. This tool is dedicated to all early childhood educators, families, and specialist teams who are working together to ensure positive, successful experiences for diverse preschool children and high-quality inclusive practice in the early years.

Acknowledgments

The Inclusive Classroom Profile (ICP™) tool would not have been possible without the expert guidance and support of a number of people. I most sincerely want to express my gratitude to:

Professor Kathy Sylva and Dr. Maria Evangelou for their multiple contributions to the preparation of the ICP. This work would have not been possible without their expert guidance on measure development and research on early childhood practice.

Dr. Pam J. Winton for her collaboration in conducting the first ICP pilot research study in the Unites States, her support for providing high-quality training on the ICP, and her ongoing efforts to expand the research and use of the ICP as a quality improvement tool. Also, Dr. Tracey West, Carla Fenson, and Lia Rucker for their thoughtful feedback on multiple drafts of the ICP. The feedback I received has been extremely helpful in guiding multiple revisions of the work.

Drs. Dick Clifford, Thelma Harms, and Debbie Cryer for their pioneering work in early childhood program quality assessment and continuous innovative contribution to the field of early childhood practice, which served as an inspiration for the development of the ICP tool and research.

Drs. Susan L. Recchia, Sam L. Odom, Sharon Ritchie, Camille Cattlet, Virginia Buysse, John Sideris, Toni Bernard, Katharina Ereky-Stevens, Iram Sirah-Blatchford, Ingrid Lunt, Julic Dockrell, Amar Dhand, Miss Sandra Mathers, and Mrs. Netta Bucket for their thought-provoking feedback on the ICP tool and research, which has strengthened the work and its possible uses.

Finally, I wish to thank all of the early childhood educators, special education teachers, program administrators, professional development providers, specialized therapists, early intervention specialists, and families of children who were involved in the development and research of the ICP. This tool was developed for them.

To Dorina and Panayotis, my first and lifetime teachers.
To Philip, Kris, and Haris, my guiding stars.

Introduction to the Inclusive Classroom Profile

The Inclusive Classroom Profile (ICP™) manual provides information about the purpose, structure, administration, and scoring of the ICP. Users are encouraged to review and become familiar with the information provided in the manual before administering the ICP. The manual is organized across four chapters. Chapter 1 is an introduction to the ICP and includes information on its purpose and uses as well as the development process and research. Chapter 2 provides an overview of the ICP items and the key practices measured by each item. Chapters 3 and 4 discuss specific guidelines for conducting an ICP assessment and scoring the ICP. Sample items are included throughout, and a Frequently Asked Questions section addresses common requests for information related to administration of the ICP.

PURPOSE AND USES OF THE ICP

The ICP is a structured observation assessment tool designed to assess the quality of daily inclusive classroom practices that support the developmental needs of children with disabilities in early childhood settings. It is designed for use in inclusive classrooms serving children ages 2–5. Ratings on the ICP items indicate the extent to which classroom practices intentionally adapt the classroom's environment, activities, and instructional supports in ways that encourage access and active participation in the group through adjustments that might differ from child to child.

High-quality inclusion is a priority across many educational systems around the world. Although universal access is still not ensured for all children from birth to age 5, international research has shown that inclusion can benefit children with and without disabilities. Specialized instruction, inclusive interventions, and supports are likely to advocate the individual learning and developmental needs of children with disabilities in early childhood programs (Odom, Buysse, & Soukakou, 2011).

The ICP was designed to contribute to international quality improvement efforts for ensuring the availability of high-quality inclusive programs. Although access to high-quality inclusion is a priority in early childhood education, there has been a lack of reliable and validated observation instruments that can be used to assess the implementation of inclusive practices aimed at improving the quality of classroom practice. The ICP was devised in response to this need to contribute a set of items that measure the quality of specific, research-based instructional and environmental supports that are thought to be necessary for meeting the needs of the diverse learning profiles of children with disabilities included in early childhood settings.

Assessors can use the ICP as a classroom quality assessment tool, as a quality improvement tool, and/or as a research instrument. When used as a quality assessment tool, the ICP is designed to assess the quality of key dimensions of classroom practice through a single assessment. Results from the ICP ratings can be used to measure the overall quality of inclusive practices in a classroom, gather assessment information on different aspects of quality, and compare quality across various types of early childhood programs (e.g., child care, public or private preschool programs).

When used as a quality improvement tool, the ICP can be a formative assessment to guide quality improvement efforts in early childhood inclusive programs. Assessment data gathered by the ICP can inform models of professional development that support those involved in meeting the needs of children with disabilities in inclusive settings. The ICP can also be used to assess the effectiveness of professional development models and interventions.

When used as a research instrument, the ICP can measure and compare quality across various types of programs, study the effectiveness of professional development interventions, and investigate the relationship between classroom quality and various characteristics related to the child, program, staff, and environment.

Although the ICP can be used independently, it can also be applied in conjunction with other early childhood environment rating scales and measures of program quality that have adequate research support. Using the ICP alongside other program quality assessment tools will enable assessors to gather information on additional dimensions of program quality (e.g., program structure, leadership, professional development). Program aspects that extend beyond the classroom, such as leadership, opportunities for professional development, and interagency collaboration, are not the focus of an ICP assessment. Similarly, curricula or interventions related to specific curriculum areas such as math, literacy, and science are not assessed by the ICP.

DEVELOPMENT OF THE ICP

Developing the ICP involved a multistep and iterative process that took place in five phases: 1) exploratory research, 2) conceptualization, 3) item generation, 4) expert review, and 5) piloting.

Exploratory Research

Development of the ICP items was guided by exploratory multiple case study research, a review of the international literature, and research on early childhood inclusion. Case study research involved nonparticipant observations in inclusive classrooms as well as interviews with practitioners, specialists, support staff, and program administrators. Review of the international literature included inclusive policies, program quality standards, measures of program and classroom quality, recommended practices in early childhood, and research studies of various aspects of inclusive practice in early childhood (e.g., Booth & Ainscow, 2002; Bredekamp & Copple, 1997; Buysse, 2011; Division for Early Childhood [DEC]/National Association for the Education of Young Children [NAEYC], 2009; Harms, Clifford, & Cryer, 2005; Irwin, 2005; Pianta, La Paro, & Hamre, 2008; Sandall, Hemmeter, Smith, & McLean, 2005; Sylva, Siraj-Blatchford, & Taggart, 2003; Wolery, Pauca, Brashers, & Grant, 2000). Review of the research focused on a broad range of dimensions related to the quality of early childhood inclusive classrooms. Areas that were reviewed included research on environmental adaptations, instructional strategies and supports, assistive technology, adult–child and peer relationships, embedded learning intervention, program structure, tiered models of intervention, assessment and progress monitoring, teaming and collaboration, family–program partnerships, and teacher attitudes and competencies (e.g., Buysse & Hollingsworth, 2009; National Professional Development Center on Inclusion, 2011; Odom et al., 2004, 2011).

Conceptualization

The concept of inclusive practices in the ICP embodies the idea of individualization within inclusive contexts. It was pivotal to the development of the items in the ICP because this concept views *quality* as a reflection of the extent to which adjustments of various elements of the classroom environment and adult support can accommodate individual needs while also encouraging children's active participation in the group (Soukakou, 2012). *Inclusive practices* from this perspective are defined as classroom-level practices that intentionally adapt the classroom's environment, activities, and instructional supports in ways that encourage access and active participation in the group, through adjustments that might differ from child to child.

Identifying a broad set of research-based goals for children with and without disabilities participating in early childhood programs was the first step in conceptualizing inclusive classroom practices. Identifying meaningful goals enabled the conceptualization of specific classroom practices that could support those goals. Specifically, inclusive practices in the ICP aim to support the following desired goals for young children and their families:

- Children's active engagement in activities and routines

- Children's knowledge and acquisition of skills across various developmental areas (e.g., language and social-communication, social-emotional development, problem solving and reasoning)

- Children's development of positive, sustained relationships with adults and peers

- Children's motivation to learn

- Children's independent learning and engagement

- Children's sense of belonging and membership in the classroom and school community

- Families' access to services and supports

- Families' understanding and involvement in children's assessment, learning, and development.

These goals have been highlighted in the international early childhood and early childhood special education literature and represent current recommended goals across international organizations, national curricula, and program guidance material (Buysse & Bailey, 1993; DEC/NAEYC, 2009; Department for Education and Standards Testing Agency, 2013; DEC, 2014; Early Childhood Outcomes Center, 2005; Odom et al., 2004).

The conceptual framework of the ICP is also aligned with the DEC/NAEYC (2009) joint position statement on inclusion, which defines a high-quality inclusive program along three key features: 1) access to a wide range of activities and environments, 2) participation that is enabled through various instructional approaches, and 3) an infrastructure of system-levels supports. According to the DEC/NAEYC joint position statement, "The desired results of inclusive experiences for children with and without disabilities and their families include a sense of belonging and membership, positive social relationships and friendships, and development and learning to reach their full potential" (p. 2). The ICP assesses the quality of practices that support desired results, such as the goals included in the joint position statement.

In addition, the DEC recommended practices (Sandall et al., 2005) was one of the many sources that helped form the development process of the ICP. The ICP quality indicators are consistent with the revised DEC recommended practices (DEC, 2014) and are based on practices that support important developmental outcomes for young children with disabilities and their families. With respect to the areas of practice, the ICP tool measures practices at the classroom level and is conceptually aligned with the following topical areas of the DEC recommended practices—assessment, environment, family, instruction, interaction, teaming, and collaboration.

Item Generation

The development of the ICP quality indicators was based on the best available research as well as on the accumulated knowledge and experience in the fields of early intervention and early childhood special education. Information gathered from case study research, review of the literature on early childhood inclusion, and expert reviews was synthesized, providing the foundation for generating quality indicators. The item generation process involved four steps. The first step involved triangulating case study research data with the literature to generate a set of dimensions of quality. The second step involved operationalizing each dimension by breaking it down into concrete, measureable quality indicators. The third step in the development process involved applying specific criteria to quality indicators to enable reliable measurement through structured observation, interview, and documentation review. The fourth step involved mapping the gradual incline of the quality indicators on a 7-point scale. Quality indicators were piloted in a small, pre-pilot sample of preschool programs ($n = 5$) prior to field-testing the ICP items in a larger sample ($n = 45$). See Soukakou (2007, 2012) and Soukakou and Sylva (2010) for a detailed description of each of the steps involved in developing the ICP items.

Expert Review

Expert review during the development of the ICP entailed submitting the newly developed measure for review to assess the content and structure of the ICP. Five reviewers included a professor of early childhood education, a professor of early childhood special education, an early childhood practitioner, and two expert researchers in measure development. Reviewers ($m = 4$) rated the importance of each of the ICP items on a 5-point scale (ranging from 1 = Not important to 5 = Very important). The means of all item ratings ranged between 4 (Important) and 5 (Very important), with 75% of the ratings scoring above a mean rating of 4.5, suggesting that experts rated the items and quality indicators as highly important inclusive practices. Reviewers ($m = 5$) also completed an open-ended questionnaire on the scale's content, structure, and administration and provided feedback that was used to revise the criteria for rating quality indicators prior to piloting and formally field-testing the measure (Soukakou, 2012).

RESEARCH ON RELIABILITY AND VALIDITY OF THE ICP

Two research studies were designed to field-test the ICP and assess its psychometric properties. In the first study, the ICP was field-tested in 45 inclusive preschool classrooms in the United Kingdom (Soukakou, 2012). A second study field-tested the ICP in classrooms in the United States. In this second study, the ICP was administered in 51 inclusive preschool classrooms in one state (Soukakou et al., 2014).

The United Kingdom Pilot Study

The ICP was field-tested in 45 inclusive preschool classrooms in the United Kingdom (Soukakou, 2012). In this sample, 112 children ranging in age from 30 months to 72 months (mean age, 50 months) had an identified disability. Data were collected by the ICP author and a trained researcher with experience in early childhood program quality assessment. Interrater reliability was assessed in a separate set of classrooms ($n = 10$), and results indicated that the independent observers were highly consistent in their ratings of individual items, with a mean weighted kappa score for the scale's items being 0.79. Cronbach's alpha analysis was conducted on the scale's items and assessed the measure's internal consistency ($\alpha = 0.79$). The factor structure of the ICP was tested through confirmatory factor analysis. The one factor model filled the assumptions and showed good values for model fit; model fit indices were $\chi^2 = 35.164$, $df = 35$, $p = .460$, $CMIN/df = 1.005$, $RMSEA = .010$, $NNFI = .998$, and $CFI = .998$. The ICP was compared with the following measures of program quality to assess construct validity: The Early Childhood Environment Rating Scale-Revised (ECERS-R; Harms et al., 2005), the Early Childhood Environment Rating Scale-Extension (ECERS-E; Sylva et al., 2003), and the Caregiver

Interaction Scale (CIS; Arnett, 1989). The total score of the ICP showed a moderately high correlation (0.626 [$p < 0.001$]) with the ECERS-R (Harms et al., 2005), suggesting that the two instruments are measuring similar, but not identical constructs (Soukakou, 2012; Soukakou & Sylva, 2010). A pattern of higher and lower correlations between the total ICP score and constructs from the other measures provided initial support for the convergent and divergent validity of the ICP. A detailed description of this validation study is reported elsewhere (Soukakou, 2012).

The North Carolina Pilot Study

The second pilot study field-tested the ICP in a sample from the United States in which the ICP was administered in 51 inclusive preschool classrooms in North Carolina (Soukakou et al., 2014). Assessors ($n = 4$) who collected the data for the validation study were experienced in conducting program quality assessments for North Carolina's Star Rated License. Assessors received training from the ICP author in using the ICP prior to data collection, and each assessor met a reliability proficiency standard of 85% agreement within 1 scale point, maintained for three consecutive reliability observations against the ICP administration and scoring standards. The mean interrater agreement across assessors was 98%, with a range of 91%–100%. Interrater agreement was further assessed in nine additional reliability-paired observations (18% of the sample) distributed over a 4-month data collection period. The mean interrater agreement across observations was 87% (within 1 point difference on the 7-point scale). Reliability at the item level was assessed using an intraclass correlation, a method for comparing raters when the measure is ordinal or interval level (Shrout & Fleiss, 1979). The mean interrater agreement was 0.71, with levels of agreement for individual items falling within an acceptable range (0.51–0.99).

Exploratory factor analysis provided evidence for a single factor solution confirming previous research results. Examination of the scree plot showed a large drop in the eigenvalue for a single factor to that for two factors, from 4.67 to 1.28. A parallel analysis was also conducted to compare the model eigenvalues with those of a set of random data (Patil, Singh, Mishra, & Donavan, 2007). According to this analysis, the number of factors that can be retained is determined by the point at which the model explains more variance than the random data. Figure 1.1 presents the scree plot and parallel analysis in support of a single factor solution. Changes for the addition of factors after the first factor were all less than 0.31. Based on this analysis, all items were retained in the final solution. Table 1.1 presents the factor loadings.

Internal consistency Cronbach's alpha analysis for the 12 items suggested that the scale's items were internally consistent ($\alpha = 0.88$). Construct validity was assessed through correlation analysis between the ratings on the ICP and ratings on the ECERS-R (Harms et al., 2005). A moderately high correlation between the total score of the ICP and the ECERS-R ($r = 0.48$) confirmed initial evidence for the construct validity of the scale (Soukakou et al., 2014). This study also explored mean differences between different types of inclusive programs using one-way analysis of variance (ANOVA). The model was significant, $F(3, 47) = 13.77$, $p < 0.05$, and accounted for a large amount of variance, $R^2 = 0.47$, indicating that differences in program type accounted for nearly half of the variance in ICP scores. Child care

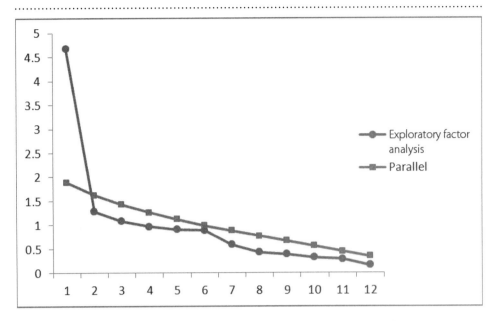

Figure 1.1.   Scree plot for Inclusive Classroom Profile (ICP) factor model and parallel analysis.

programs scored significantly lower than other programs included in the sample (i.e., development day programs, Head Start, public pre-K programs).

This study gathered additional data on the usability of the ICP and the quality of the training program. Four assessors with experience in conducting program quality assessments for a Star Rated License program in North Carolina provided ratings on a social validity assessment (1- to 5-point rating scale) by evaluating the quality of the training they received, the importance of the ICP items, and the ease of use of the ICP tool (a score of 1 representing the lowest rating, and a score of 5

Table 1.1.   Factor loadings

Item	Factor loadings
ICP 1: Adaptations of space, materials, and equipment	0.47
ICP 2: Adult involvement in peer interactions	0.58
ICP 3: Adults' guidance of children's free-choice activities and play	0.72
ICP 4: Conflict resolution	0.49
ICP 5: Membership	0.48
ICP 6: Relationships between adults and children	0.84
ICP 7: Support for communication	0.64
ICP 8: Adaptations of group activities	0.51
ICP 9: Transitions between activities	0.34
ICP 10: Feedback	0.70
ICP 11: Family–professional partnerships	0.38
ICP 12: Monitoring children's learning	0.62

Key: ICP = Inclusive Classroom Profile

representing the highest rating). Results indicated that assessors rated the importance of the constructs measured by the ICP very highly ($m = 5$), reported that that they would highly recommend the ICP measure to others ($m = 5$), and found the measure easy to administer ($m = 4$). With regard to the training program, assessors rated the ICP overview training session on administration and scoring as useful ($m = 3.75$) and reported that they felt well prepared after the reliability training observations ($m = 4$; Soukakou et al., 2014). A detailed description of the study's results can be found in Soukakou et al. (2014).

USING THE ICP TO SUPPORT QUALITY IMPROVEMENT

The ICP was designed as an assessment tool that could be used by early educators, professional development providers, and program administrators aiming to improve the quality of inclusion in early childhood settings. Although there is consensus on the importance of having a qualified and effective early childhood work force in inclusive settings, there is less agreement on how to support early educators in consistently implementing high-quality inclusive practices (National Professional Development Center on Inclusion, 2008). Current data suggest that the majority of early childhood personnel are not adequately prepared to implement instructional and curricular adaptations that are needed for meeting the individual learning needs of young children with disabilities and for ensuring early school success (Chang, Early, & Winton, 2005; Early & Winton, 2001; Hyson, Horm, & Winton, 2012). Moreover, some evidence suggests that in-service early childhood teachers do not receive adequate support to feel competent or confident in implementing inclusive practices (Buysse, Wesley, Keyes, & Bailey, 1996). In this context, programs and policy makers face significant challenges in their efforts to plan professional development approaches and strategies that can result in long-lasting changes in classroom practice (Zaslow, Tout, Halle, Whittaker, & Lavelle, 2010). The lack of reliable and valid assessment tools that can be used to guide professional development programs that support inclusion is a key challenge.

Guiding quality improvement efforts by linking assessment data with instructional decision making is one of the ICP's uses. As a formative assessment tool, the ICP can be used as part of a professional development program that involves highly qualified professional development providers and research-based inclusive practices as the content of professional development and incorporates effective coaching and consultation strategies for supporting learners in implementing inclusive practices. Efforts are under way by the author of the ICP and international research teams to develop a professional development program that includes the ICP as a centerpiece.

Structure of the ICP

The ICP is a structured observation rating scale organized around 12 practices or items that have the strongest research base for supporting the education and development of young children with disabilities in inclusive settings.

1. Adaptations of space, materials, and equipment

2. Adult involvement in peer interactions

3. Adults' guidance of children's free-choice activities and play

4. Conflict resolution

5. Membership

6. Relationships between adults and children

7. Support for communication

8. Adaptations of group activities

9. Transitions between activities

10. Feedback

11. Family–professional partnerships

12. Monitoring children's learning

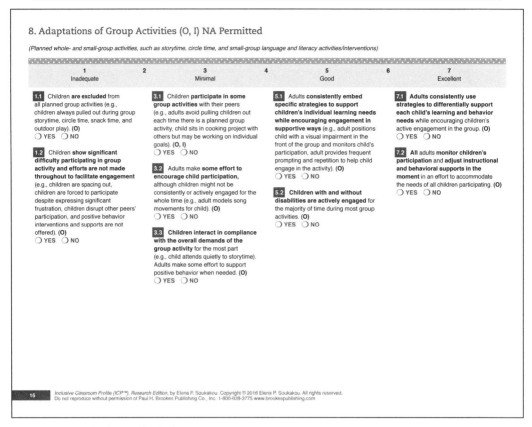

Figure 2.1. Example of Item with criteria page.

ICP items are assessed on a 7-point rating scale that rates the quality of classroom practices ranging from 1 (practices considered highly inadequate for promoting children's active participation in the group and meeting their individual needs) to 7 (practices that promote to the highest degree children's active participation in the group through individualized strategies and accommodations). Each item comprises a set of quality indicators under the form of qualitative descriptions of various practices (see Figure 2.1). Each quality indicator includes specific examples that illustrate the various ways in which that particular practice at that level of quality can be performed. Finally, each item page is accompanied by a separate page that lists the criteria for rating

Criteria for Rating Indicators

Item 8 assesses the quality of adaptations during whole- and small-group activities that are structured, led by an adult, and require children's participation. Examples include circle time, storybook reading, group cooking, music and art activities, and adult-led small-group language/literacy activities and interventions. A small-group activity initiated by children during free-choice activity and playtime is not considered in this item. NA is permitted if no group activities are observed on the day of the assessment, if the program does not involve any planned group activities, or if only one group activity was observed and children were intentionally pulled out of the classroom for one-to-one therapy.

3.1 Score YES if all children participate in at least one daily group activity with their peers (other than snack time) during the day. If a child is intentionally pulled out of a group activity to participate in a different group or one-to-one activity in the classroom (e.g., small-group intervention with two to three children, one-to-one activity with a teacher), then you may still score YES if the activity was intentionally planned to meet individual learning goals. You can interview the teacher in such cases. Ask, "Do children participate in daily planned activities?" Continue your question to find out more about the purpose and intention to remove a child from a whole-group activity. Do not give credit if children are removed from group activities and allowed to wander around in the classroom as a result of adults' lack of effort to support children's engagement during group activities.

3.2 If at least one child is not engaged for the majority of the time, and no efforts were made to support participation, then do not give credit.

5.1 Score YES if you observe several examples used with the majority of children to support active and sustained participation in the activity. Adaptations can be made in the 1) materials, physical space, and equipment (e.g., use of visual props, adaptive equipment, thicker brush); 2) objectives, structure, and grouping (e.g., while other children are drawing shapes, one child's goal is to trace a circle); or 3) instructional

support (e.g., offering hand-over-hand assistance, modeling for child how to perform an activity, adapting directions and prompts, repeating instructions). This indicator does not assess how groups are formed. Observe groups, including groups only of children with disabilities). You can also score YES if no adaptations were observed and all children with disabilities seemed actively engaged for 85% or more of the activity time. If a child had to be removed from a group activity for behavior support or joined a different small group or one-to-one activity/intervention in the classroom, then consider the previous examples of strategies for supporting engagement.

5.2 Score YES if the majority of the children under observation and the majority of the rest of the group are actively engaged most of the time.

7.1 Score YES if children with disabilities are actively engaged and adults are available to provide individualized support for every child, if needed. Also, score YES if a child has difficulty participating in the group, but adults consistently use strategies to support his or her needs (e.g., child runs away during group activity and adult gradually uses more explicit verbal and physical prompts to encourage child participation). Score NO if at least one child has difficulty participating in a group activity and adults do not consistently accommodate his or her needs to facilitate participation.

NOTES _____

_____

_____

_____

_____

_____

_____

17

Figure 2.1. *(continued)*

the quality indicators of that particular item. The criteria are designed to help assessors accurately and consistently rate items.

ICP ITEMS

This section presents an overview of the 12 ICP items. Each ICP item's profile outlines the key practices that are being assessed by the item's quality indicators and provides the method for gathering assessment information (i.e., observation, interview, documentation review). A brief description of each item is provided at the top of each page labeled "criteria for rating indicators."

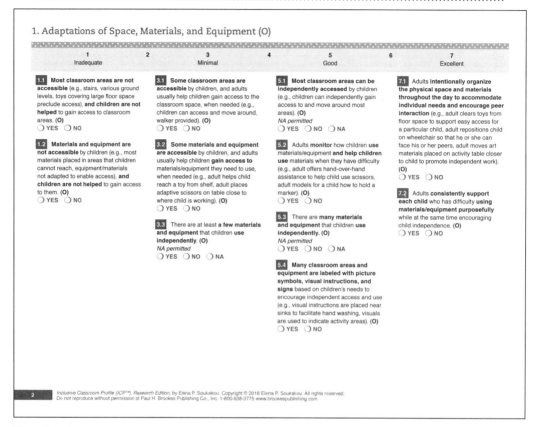

Figure 2.2.   Item 1

ITEM 1: Adaptations of Space, Materials, and Equipment

Item 1 (see Figure 2.2) assesses the quality of environmental adaptations and adult strategies for supporting children's access and use of the classroom's physical space, equipment, and materials. It also assesses the extent to which adults intentionally organize the physical space and materials during the day to support children's learning and social experience. Assessment of Item 1 practices considers both indoor and outdoor space that is used by the children on the day of the assessment.

What Does This Item Assess?

- Children's access to classroom physical space, materials, and equipment

- Adult support for gaining access to and using the classroom's space, materials, and equipment

- Environmental arrangements for supporting children's individual learning and social experience

- Adult support for promoting independent access and use of space, materials, and equipment

Criteria for Rating Indicators

Item 1 assesses the quality of environmental adaptations and adult strategies for supporting children's access to and use of the classroom's physical space, materials, and equipment. It also assesses the extent to which adults intentionally organize and adjust the physical space and materials during the day to support children's learning and social experience. Assessment of Item 1 practices considers both indoor and outdoor space that is used by the children on the day of the assessment.

1.2 Accessible = available at an area where a child can get it independently (e.g., on shelves where children can reach, located within view of children, labeled so that children know what they are).

3.3 Score YES if the majority of the children used at least a few materials and equipment independently during the observation time. NA is permitted if children's physical or mental ability is so impaired that they cannot use any materials independently.

5.1 Score YES if the space is organized or adapted in such way that it enables most children to gain access to most areas of the classroom independently. This indicator does not apply to children whose motor ability is so limited that they cannot gain access to most areas independently. NA is permitted in this case.

5.2 Score YES if the majority of children are helped most of the time, when needed, although support across children may not be provided consistently across all children. Do not give credit if at least one child is not consistently supported when adult support is needed.

5.3 Score YES if the majority of the children used many materials and equipment independently during the observation. Observe if materials are placed, organized, and labeled in ways that enable children in the room to use them independently. It is possible that some children can use many materials independently but may choose not to on the day of your visit. This may be due, however, to a lack of appropriate adaptations, accessibility of materials, or lack of support for independent use. Therefore, in cases in which the majority of children you observe do not use many materials and equipment independently, you can give credit only if you observe adults encouraging children to use different materials independently. NA is permitted if children's physical or mental ability is so impaired that they cannot use many materials independently.

7.1 Score YES if you observe at least one to two clear examples with one or across children demonstrating that environmental arrangements are made to support children's individual needs and social experience, when needed. Do not give credit if you observe several missed opportunities to promote such goals through environmental modifications.

7.2 Score YES if each child is consistently supported in using materials and equipment, when needed.

NOTES _____

Figure 2.2. *(continued)*

How Is Assessment Information Gathered?

• Observation

What Does It Look Like in a High-Quality Inclusive Classroom?

Children with and without disabilities in Kelly's preschool inclusive classroom can gain access to the physical space, materials, and equipment. Children are helped, when needed, not only to gain access to but also to use materials in meaningful ways through adult scaffolding strategies. Kelly and her teacher assistants set up the classroom areas and materials in ways that can be accessible to all children, but they dynamically organize the physical space, equipment, and materials throughout the day to intentionally encourage children's independence and social interactions between peers, and meet each child's individual needs. For example, Kelly observed Tara, a 4-year-old child with cerebral palsy, use her walker this morning to walk from the block corner toward the art area during free playtime. Kelly intentionally prompted Tara's peers at the block corner to clear the alley next to the block corner by removing some toys so that Tara could independently gain access to the space.

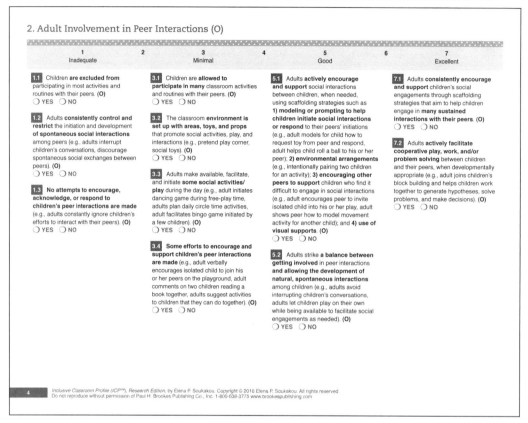

Figure 2.3. Item 2

ITEM 2: Adult Involvement in Peer Interactions

Item 2 (see Figure 2.3) assesses the quality of activities and strategies implemented to support children's social experience and development of positive, sustained relationships with their peers.

What Does This Item Assess?

- Opportunities for children to participate in activities and routines with their peers

- Adult planning of daily social play and learning activities

- Adult facilitation of daily social activities and play

- Adult scaffolding strategies for supporting positive, reciprocal, sustained peer interactions and relationships between children

- Balance between adult involvement and support for children's spontaneous social engagements

- Adult facilitation of problem solving between children

Criteria for Rating Indicators

Item 2 assesses the quality of activities and strategies implemented to support children's social experience and development of positive, sustained relationships with their peers.

3.4   Score YES if at least two examples of adult support are observed with each child showing difficulty in engaging and sustaining peer interactions. Adult encouragement and responsiveness can be observed with individual children (e.g., adult encourages child to join his or her peers in play) or within a group context (e.g., at the end of circle time, adult suggests social games for children to play together). You may still give credit if the children were observed sustaining many peer interactions, and, therefore, minimal or no scaffolding was needed.

5.1   Score YES if many examples are observed throughout the day with the majority of children showing peer interaction difficulties, although support may not always be consistently provided for each child. Other peers can include both children with and without identified disabilities.

7.1   Score YES if you observe adults intentionally and consistently supporting children to sustain social interactions throughout the day. You may still give credit in cases in which the children observed required minimal or no adult facilitation to sustain peer interactions

or in cases in which one or more children demonstrated significant difficulty relating to other peers, and adults intentionally and consistently supported their interactions. Do not give credit, however, if at least one child showed difficulty engaging and sustaining peer interactions and individualized strategies for helping the child were not observed. Adults might use various strategies (see 5.1) to support children in sustaining reciprocal peer interactions (e.g., adult continuously uses verbal prompts to help a child sustain conversation with peer, adult facilitates a group table game by demonstrating how to take turns throughout the game).

7.2   You can score YES if it was evident that the children observed could not engage in cooperative problem solving or play and, therefore, encouraging it seemed inappropriate. Do not give credit, however, if several missed opportunities were observed to facilitate group discussion and collaborative problem solving among two or more children. The importance of this practice is the process of intentionally helping children to think, problem-solve, work, and play collaboratively (e.g., learn how to listen to others' thoughts, build on others' ideas, solve problems cooperatively, work toward common goals).

NOTES _____

Figure 2.3. *(continued)*

How Is Assessment Information Gathered?

• Observation

What Does It Look Like in a High-Quality Inclusive Classroom?

Kelly's classroom is set up with areas, toys, and props that promote social activities, social play, and interactions (e.g., pretend play corner, social toys), and adults plan and implement social activities across various routines throughout the day. Adults consistently encourage and support children's social engagements in the classroom through scaffolding strategies such as modeling for a child how to engage in play with his or her peer, using verbal prompting to help a child sustain his or her play with his or her peer, and enlisting other peers to support particular children who have difficulty engaging in peer interactions. For example, during circle time, Kelly invited Andrew to model for Peter, a 3-year-old child who is nonverbal and has a developmental delay, the movements of a song he likes to perform with his peers. Watching Andrew use his hands to form the movements of the song has been an effective way to help Peter imitate, learn, and perform the song movements independently.

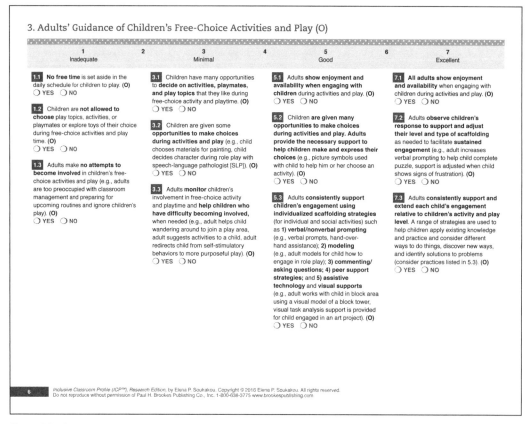

Figure 2.4.   Item 3

ITEM 3: Adults' Guidance of Children's Free-Choice Activities and Play

Item 3 (see Figure 2.4) assesses the quality of practices that are aimed at supporting children's engagement in both individual and social activities and play. Assessment of Item 3 considers practices that are implemented during the time when children can engage in play and various individual and social activities of their choice (considers all activities other than planned group times).

What Does This Item Assess?

- Opportunities for children to participate in a variety of learning activities and play of their choice

- Opportunities for children to make choices, and adult support for helping children understand, develop, and communicate their choices

- Adult use of scaffolding strategies for supporting children's active engagement in activities and play

- Adult availability and enjoyment when engaging with children

- Adult support for extending children's learning and play skills

Criteria for Rating Indicators

Item 3 assesses the quality of practices that are aimed at supporting children's engagement in both individual and social activities and play. Assessment of Item 3 considers practices that are implemented during the time when children can engage in play and various individual and social activities of their choice (consider all activities other than planned group times). Activities might be organized across various choice centers of the classroom, such as a make-believe play area, a book-reading corner, a blocks/construction center, a sand table, or a writing center.

3.1 You can score YES if one child is engaged in a structured activity as part of planned intervention throughout your observation time (e.g., child is engaged in structured play therapy with a therapist for a large part of the free-choice time) as long as the weekly planning shows that all children have many daily opportunities in the week to participate in activities and play of their choice.

3.3 Score YES if adults observe children's involvement in play and intervene to help children choose and start their play. Do not give credit if at least one child cannot become involved and adults do not attempt to help him or her become involved (e.g., child is wandering around play areas, child moves from one activity center to another not knowing how to initiate play or what to do with the toys and materials).

5.1 This can be expressed through sustained warm comments, smiles, or engaging gestures. The majority of adults show enjoyment and availability throughout the day.

5.2 Score YES if children are encouraged to make many choices related to their activities, play, and learning. Adults not only offer children opportunities to make choices, but also help them understand and express their decisions. Do not give credit if you observe at least one child showing difficulty making a choice and is not helped in communicating his or his choices.

5.3 Score YES if you observe many examples of one or more recommended strategies across the majority of children used to help support or extend their individual and social play. Support needs to be consistently provided across the day's activities for the majority of children who have difficulty organizing or sustaining their play. Some children may need less scaffolding, depending on their developmental level and type of play (while

a child spends most of the time focused on completing his or her LEGO construction, an adult monitors the child's engagement and at times moves closer to comment or ask questions about his or her construction). Do not give credit if at least one child has difficulty engaging in play/activities and no efforts to help him or her remain engaged are observed. Examples of visual supports include picture schedules, visual maps, and picture symbols. Different children might benefit from different types of strategies. Additional examples of scaffolding strategies might include

- Withholding access of toys and props to encourage children to make requests and communicate with others about their play
- Using wait time (deliberately waiting a few seconds for a child to initiate an interaction, make a choice, or respond)
- Gradually increasing and decreasing assistance to support children's play (e.g., gradually decreasing verbal prompts when helping a child do a puzzle)

7.2 Sustained engagement: child remains actively engaged in the play he or she has purposefully orchestrated. Time of engagement may vary across children. Score YES if you observe continuous, intentional efforts to help children sustain their play (see examples of strategies listed in 5.3) or if the majority of children were actively engaged in sustained, purposeful play for the majority of the free-play/activity time. Some children might have difficulty sustaining their engagement (e.g., child can sustain his or her play only for brief periods), and, therefore, a rating should reflect the quality of adult support provided to help children sustain their activity. Do not give credit if at least one child has difficulty sustaining his or her play and no efforts were observed to support his or her engagement.

Figure 2.4. *(continued)*

How Is Assessment Information Gathered?

- Observation

What Does It Look Like in a High-Quality Inclusive Classroom?

All of the adults in Kelly's classroom show enjoyment and availability when engaging with children during activities and play. Children have many opportunities to decide on activities, playmates, and play topics that they like during free-choice activity, and they are given many opportunities to make choices during activities and playtime. Adults in this classroom observe children's engagement in play and consistently support children's play using individualized strategies such as verbal/nonverbal prompting, modeling, commenting/ asking questions, enlisting other peers, and using assistive technology and visual supports (e.g., adult uses a visual map to help a child begin, perform, and complete an activity). Kelly joined Martha, a 4-year-old girl who was recently diagnosed with autism, during free-choice time. Kelly used a visual activity organizer in the role-play area to help Martha act out the steps involved in cooking a meal for her friends.

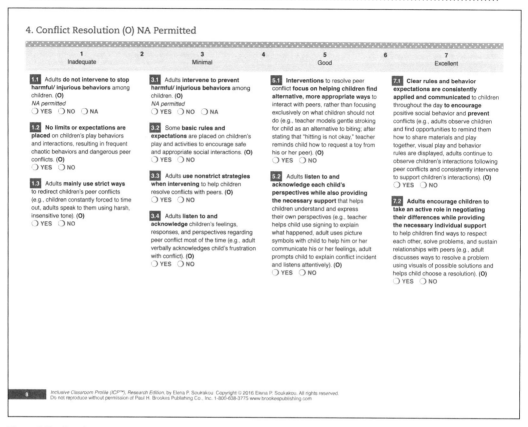

Figure 2.5.   Item 4

ITEM 4: Conflict Resolution

This item (see Figure 2.5) assesses the quality of adult support during incidents of observed peer conflict as well as practices for preventing persisting peer conflict.

What Does This Item Assess?

- Adult provisions and strategies to prevent and mediate peer conflict

- Adult communicating clear expectations as a strategy for promoting positive social engagements

- Adult acknowledging children's perspectives and helping children communicate their perspectives on peer conflict incidents

- Adult promotion of alternative, positive behaviors and functional solutions

- Adult's use of individualized strategies for helping children negotiate peer conflict and generate solutions

How Is Assessment Information Gathered?

- Observation

Criteria for Rating Indicators

Item 4 assesses the quality of adult support during incidents of observed peer conflict as well as practices for preventing persisting peer conflict. Most indicators are scored once an adult has intervened to support children's peer interactions. Minor incidents of peer conflict (e.g., child attempts to grab a toy from his or her peer and then leaves) that do not result in adult intervention are not rated here. Failing to intervene to prevent harmful/injurious behaviors is rated by indicators 1.1 and 3.1. NA is permitted for the item if no examples of peer conflict are observed during the ICP assessment.

1.1   NA is applicable if no harmful/injurious behaviors are observed.

1.3   Score YES if strict approaches are observed with at least one child observed in the classroom.

3.1   NA is applicable if no harmful/injurious behaviors are observed.

3.4   Score YES if adults listened to or acknowledged children's feelings/perspectives in most of the observed incidents (two out of two incidents or in more than 50% when more than two incidents were observed).

5.2   Score YES if the perspectives of all children involved in conflict were considered most of the time, if possible. Adults may need to use alternative means of communication, concrete objects, visuals, and materials, such as puppets, photographs, or storybooks, for some children who might have difficulty understanding others' feelings and perspectives or who may have difficulty communicating their own perspectives to their peers (e.g., adult shows visual symbol for *angry* to child and says, "I can see you are angry. Do you want to tell me what happened?" Adult shows child pictures of faces

expressing different emotions and helps child identify a picture to communicate how he or she feels toward his or her peer).

7.1   This indicator assesses the extent to which adults are consistent about the rules and behaviors they expect from children and the extent to which adults intentionally monitor children's interactions in an effort to be proactive about peer conflict. In classrooms where minimal conflict was observed, you can score YES if adults seemed alert about children's peer interactions but did not have to remind children of various behavior rules other than what they did to get credit for 5.1 (intervened during conflict and pointed out alternative, more positive ways to interact). Do not give credit, however, if you observe an incident of persistent peer conflict during which adults may have intervened, as 5.1 requires, but then ignored children, allowing conflict to persist and escalate dangerously. Also, do not give credit if you observe many incidents of peer conflict and adults missed many opportunities throughout the day to remind, model for children, or explain various classroom, activity, and behavioral expectations to children. Adults may intervene, as 5.1 requires, but this may not be enough for many children; children may need to be monitored more closely and reminded and supported more frequently during the day.

NOTES _____

Figure 2.5. *(continued)*

What Does It Look Like in a High-Quality Inclusive Classroom?

Adults in Kelly's classroom have set clear rules and behavioral expectations that are consistently communicated to children throughout the day to encourage positive social behavior and prevent conflicts. For example, adults intentionally observe children's interactions during free playtime and, when needed, remind children of various play rules and ways of positively interacting with their peers in an effort to prevent conflicts. When children seem to have difficulty resolving their differences on their own, adults join children to listen to all children's perspectives, acknowledging their views and feelings. They also try to focus on helping children find alternative, more positive ways for negotiating their differences. For example, Kelly observed two children on the playground fighting over a new toy. She invited the two children to consider different, more positive ways by which they could both enjoy the new toy. One of the two children involved in the conflict had a communication difficulty in the area of expressive language, and, therefore, Kelly invited the children to look at some visuals that depicted possible, alternative solutions. With Kelly's facilitation, the two children decided to take turns using the new toy by paying attention to an alarm clock that would guide them when to pass the toy to each other.

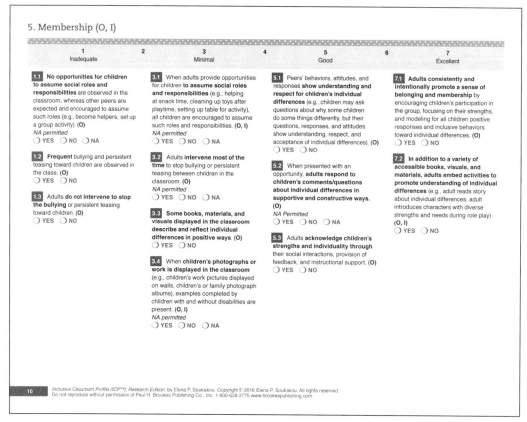

Figure 2.6.   Item 5

ITEM 5: Membership

Item 5 (see Figure 2.6) measures the quality of practices that promote equal opportunities for children to assume various roles and responsibilities in the classroom, a sense of belonging, and a social climate in which individual differences are recognized and accepted.

What Does This Item Assess?

- Opportunities for children to assume equal roles and responsibilities in the classroom

- Adult interventions for preventing bullying or persistent teasing between children in the classroom

- Adult use of positive and inclusive strategies for responding to children's individual differences

- Adult use of resources for promoting acceptance and understanding of individual differences

Criteria for Rating Indicators

Item 5 measures the quality of practices that promote equal opportunities for children to assume various roles and responsibilities in the classroom, a sense of belonging, and a social climate in which individual differences are accepted and understood.

3.1   Social roles and responsibilities might include helping set up the table for snack or activity, cleaning up toys/food, and assigning child to be the helper for the day. Score YES if at least one example is observed when an opportunity is given for all children to assume a responsibility. Score NO if it is evident from the observation that children with disabilities are not given equal opportunities (e.g., children with disabilities are not encouraged to clean up their snacks). NA is permitted if assuming social responsibilities is not part of a classroom's routines and, therefore, not observed for any child in the classroom. NA is also permitted if a child's observed disability precludes him or her from assuming such roles when opportunities are offered to the group. If the only example observed involved asking a child (not one of the children under observation) to assume a social role (e.g., become a helper for the day), then you can score this indicator by looking for evidence posted in the classroom that demonstrates that all children assume similar roles at different times (e.g., names of weekly helpers and dates are displayed in the classroom). Or, you can also interview the teacher. Ask, "Do all children in the classroom have equal opportunities to assume roles?" Score YES if teacher confirms and provides an example that explains how they encourage all children to assume particular roles or responsibilities.

3.3   At least three to four examples are displayed in the classroom that positively reflect individual differences across diverse strengths and needs. Examples should extend beyond resources promoting cultural diversity to include resources focused on differences in learning (e.g., linguistic differences, learning differences, skills, behaviors). Examples may include photographs of children or adults with various developmental strengths and needs, stories about children's diverse learning and emotional needs, visual displays of facial expressions, and adaptive equipment.

3.4   This indicator is scored in classrooms that display and use children's photographs, work, or personal/family information in an intentional manner. Examples include a wall display of children's birthdates or heights (meaningful to children in group and not simply generic school supply type items only); photographs of children, their families, recent classroom trips, and other activities (posted on the wall or in photograph albums); display of children's art when all children are invited to display their work, such as following a theme-related project or a bulletin board art gallery; stories developed by the students; and small photographs of individual children in various activities.

Score YES if

- At least one of the previous examples is observable and the majority of the children with disabilities are represented.
- None of the previous examples are observed and the classroom includes only a few pieces of art posted on the walls. You need to interview the teacher. Ask, "How do you make decisions about children's work and photographs that are displayed in the classroom?" Score YES if teachers report that all children are allowed and invited to display pictures or their own work, but they may choose not to (e.g., a photograph album exists in the classroom in which families and children can contribute photographs by choice). It is important not to penalize a classroom that might not include children's work or personal photographs as practice (this is not the intent of this indicator) or a classroom that displays work or photographs of children only when and if they volunteer, such as if a child asks to hang his or her painting.

Score NO if at least one of the defining examples is observable and the majority of children with disabilities are not represented.

NA is permitted if

- None of the previous examples are observed, or the only photographs of children are those permanently displayed to make up the class group.
- It is evident from the observation that children's severity of disability precludes them from participating in the kind of work that is displayed.

7.2   Score YES if at least two examples of activities are observed. If you do not get to observe examples of activities, then you need to interview the teacher. Ask, "How do you help children understand each other's differences in learning, skills, or behaviors? Can you describe some activities that you might do in the classroom?" Score YES if the teacher describes at least two examples of activities. Activities need to be specific, reflect planned efforts to support understanding of individual differences, and extend beyond cultural differences.

Figure 2.6.   *(continued)*

How Is Assessment Information Gathered?

- Observation
- Interview

What Does It Look Like in a High-Quality Inclusive Classroom?

Adults in Kelly's classroom work together to create a classroom community in which all children feel that they belong in the group, regardless of their individual differences. Adults develop a sense of belonging by planning activities and creating many opportunities during the day through children's social interactions to help children understand and accept individual differences. For example, when a child asked Kelly why another child was using a spoon that was shaped different to eat with during snack time, Kelly responded that children can use different spoons as they grow and learn to eat different foods. She showed all of the children the many sizes of spoons she had available for all of the children in the group to use. Kelly showed examples of how younger children might need bigger or softer spoons and demonstrated how some spoons might be easier for some children to hold.

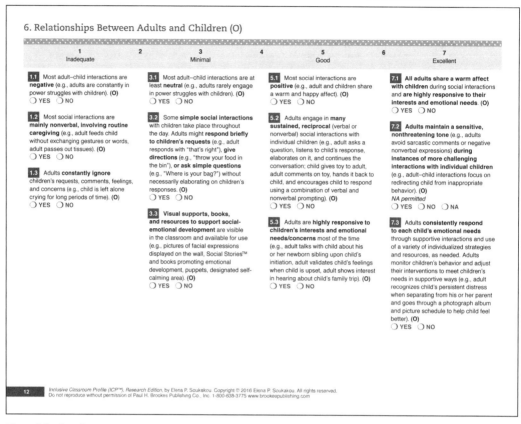

Figure 2.7.   Item 6

ITEM 6: Relationships Between Adults and Children

Item 6 (see Figure 2.7) assesses the quality of social interactions and relationships between adults and children by measuring the extent to which adults engage in responsive, reciprocal, and sustained social interactions with children.

What Does This Item Assess?

- Adult engagement in positive, reciprocal, and sustained social interactions
- Adult responsiveness to children's interests
- Adult responsiveness to children's emotional needs
- Adult support during more challenging social interactions with individual children
- Adult use of visual supports and additional classroom resources for supporting children's emotional needs and development

Criteria for Rating Indicators

Item 6 assesses the quality of social interactions and relationships between adults and children by measuring the extent to which adults engage in responsive, reciprocal, and sustained social interactions with children.

3.3   Score YES if at least three to four examples (from one or more categories) are visible in the classroom and available to use.

5.2   Score YES if many reciprocal social interactions are observed with the majority of children in which adults make intentional efforts to help children sustain interactions with them. Adult- or child-initiated social interactions need to be observed throughout the day. Adults seek opportunities to engage in interactions that are in tune with children's developmental needs and interests. Examples are found in different contexts, such as during snack time, on the playground, and at free-choice activity time.

Reciprocal is an interaction in which person A (child or adult) initiates, person B responds, and person A elaborates or continues with a comment, question, prompt, or gesture. Interactions can be verbal or nonverbal.

Sustained is at least two consecutive cycles of reciprocal interactions. Sustainability of adult–child interactions depends on children's age and abilities. Therefore, do not penalize a classroom in which a child is not capable of sustaining reciprocal interactions if adults make consistent efforts to sustain reciprocal interactions with children.

5.3   Score YES if adults are responsive most of the time with the majority of the children, although at times their responsiveness might be inconsistent with some children. Adults make efforts to accommodate children's expressed interests and ideas as well as respond to their emotional needs or expressed concerns in supportive ways. This includes children's expressed interests or concerns related to experiences outside the classroom as well (e.g., child lets teacher know about his or her new baby brother). Do not give credit if one child's interests, concerns, or frustration is consistently ignored.

7.3   Adults may not always be successful in their efforts to end children's frustration, meet their emotional needs, and ensure positive behavior. You need to observe strategies/interventions implemented in the moment to support children's feelings, emotional understanding, and positive behavior, however, to give credit. Strategies may include arranging the environment (e.g., removing a child from group time to have a gentle discussion), using visuals and supportive materials (e.g., picture symbols, puppets, transition objects), reviewing classroom expectations, having supportive conversations, and providing effort-based feedback.

NOTES _____

13

Figure 2.7.   *(continued)*

How Is Assessment Information Gathered?

- Observation

What Does It Look Like in a High-Quality Inclusive Classroom?

All adults in Kelly's classroom show enjoyment when interacting with the children. Adults seek many opportunities during the day to engage in social interactions that are positive, reciprocal, and sustained. Adults are highly responsive to children's interests as well as their emotional needs when they interact with the children. For example, when Charlie, a 4-year-old boy, seemed reluctant to play outside because of the thunder he had heard earlier in the morning during a thunderstorm, Kelly read a picture book with Charlie about thunderstorms. When they finished reading the book, Kelly modeled for Charlie all of the different things he could do if he felt uncomfortable while being outside on the playground. Kelly's shared reading activity and follow-up conversation seemed to help Charlie feel better and encouraged him to join his peers on the playground.

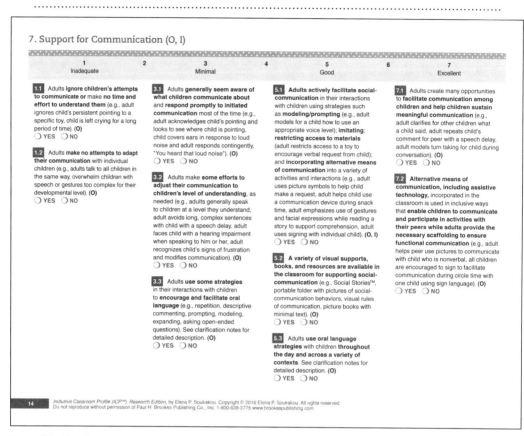

Figure 2.8.   Item 7

ITEM 7: Support for Communication

Item 7 (see Figure 2.8) assesses the quality of supports for encouraging and supporting children's language and communication skills.

What Does This Item Assess?

- Adult responsiveness to children's initiated communication

- Adult use of scaffolding strategies to encourage and facilitate social-communication

- Adult use of alternative means of communication systems and supports to facilitate communication

- Adult use of strategies for encouraging and facilitating oral language development

- Adult use of visual supports, books, and classroom resources for supporting social-communication

Criteria for Rating Indicators

Item 7 assesses the quality of supports for encouraging and supporting children's language and communication skills.

3.1   Adults may occasionally misread children's attempts to communicate, but you can score YES if they are responsive most of the time to the majority of the children and if they make some efforts to understand children.

3.2   Score YES if some efforts are observed across the majority of the children when needed to adjust communication to children's level of understanding. Adjustments in verbal interaction may include use of speech as well as paralinguistic aspects of verbal communication, such as emphasizing words and intonation.

3.3   Score YES if at least one of the following oral language strategies is used at least occasionally with the majority of children to encourage, facilitate, or model language:

- Repetition: Adult repeats or recasts own words in order to emphasize important words (e.g., adult says to child, "Do you hear the doggie? Hear the doggie? Doggie!").
- Response prompting: Adult gives verbal or nonverbal prompts to help child come up with a word, complete a sentence, or communicate an idea (e.g., "I think the word you are thinking about starts with the /g/ sound").
- Modeling: Adult demonstrates various elements of expressive language (e.g., how to ask for help) as well as other elements of social-communication (e.g., waiting for a response, adjusting pace of speaking and voice tone) for the child.
- Descriptive commenting: Adult comments on what the child appears to be attending (e.g., adult watches child painting and says, "You are painting with so many colors," adult approaches child and initiates, "Look! It's raining!").
- Expanding: Adult elaborates on what the child says. Expansions can be semantical when adult adds meaning (e.g., child says "doggie" and adult expands, "Yes, that is a big, brown doggie") or syntactical when adult extends syntax (e.g., child points to cookie saying "cookie" and adult extends with, "This is a cookie").
- Asking open-ended questions: Adult asks child a question that requires more than a one-word response and waits for child to respond.

5.1   Alternative means of communication include use of gestures, sign systems, facial expressions, speech-generating devices (SGDs), and picture symbols (e.g., Picture Exchange Communication System [PECS]). Because using certain alternative communication systems, (e.g., SGDs, PECS) often requires professional assessment, do not penalize a classroom that does not use a particular system, unless it is professionally recommended. If children were observed having difficulty communicating with adults and peers, and alternative communication systems were not observed, then you need to interview the teacher. Ask, "Are any alternative communication systems recommended for the child(ren)?" Do not give credit if adults report that an alternative communication system is professionally recommended but was not implemented. If adults report that an alternative communication system was not being professionally recommended, then consider the strategies listed in the indicator for facilitating social-communication as well as the ways in which adults incorporate nonverbal communication in their interactions with children (e.g., using gestures and picture symbols). Do not give credit if at least one child seemed to have difficulty communicating with others and his or her communication was not facilitated throughout routines, activities, and interactions.

5.2   Score YES if at least three to four different types of resources need to be observed and available for use (e.g., books, Social Stories™, visual supports for social communication).

5.3   Score YES if many examples are observed with the majority of children to support oral language throughout the day. You need to observe the use of at least three different strategies. Children are supported across many different contexts (e.g., centers, small-group activity, individual interactions, outdoor play). Do not give credit if at least one child with observed oral language difficulties was not supported during your observation time. Adults consistently use strategies with children to encourage and facilitate communication and model, expand, and build complexity into children's use of language.

Figure 2.8.   *(continued)*

- Adult support for facilitating meaningful, sustained communication between children

How Is Assessment Information Gathered?

- Observation
- Interview

What Does It Look Like in a High-Quality Inclusive Classroom?

Adults in Kelly's classroom actively facilitate social-communication in their interactions with children using a variety of scaffolding strategies including alternative means of communication systems. Adults intentionally use alternative means of communication systems in ways that enable children to communicate and participate in classroom activities with their peers. For example, Kelly showed Martha, the helper of the day, how to use picture symbols of available snacks to help Andy, a boy with a communication difficulty, make a choice of his snack. As Martha went around the table verbally asking each child to make a choice between two snacks, she used two picture cards to help Andy make his choice.

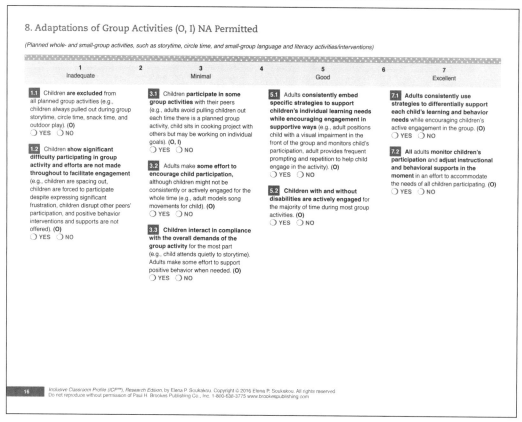

Figure 2.9. Item 8

ITEM 8: Adaptations of Group Activities

Item 8 (see Figure 2.9) measures the quality of adaptations during whole-group and small-group activities that are structured and led or facilitated by adults. Adaptations might include adjustments in the space, materials, and equipment used for activities; the structure of activities; and the instructional supports used by adults to support children's active participation in the group.

What Does This Item Assess?

- Opportunities for children to participate with their peers in planned whole-group and small-group activities

- Adult use of embedded strategies and adaptations of activities to support children's active engagement and participation while also meeting children's individual needs

- Adult planning and monitoring of embedded strategies and adaptations to support children's individual needs

Criteria for Rating Indicators

Item 8 assesses the quality of adaptations during whole- and small-group activities that are structured, led by an adult, and require children's participation. Examples include circle time, storybook reading, group cooking, music and art activities, and adult-led small-group language/literacy activities and interventions. A small-group activity initiated by children during free-choice activity and playtime is not considered in this item. NA is permitted if no group activities are observed on the day of the assessment, if the program does not involve any planned group activities, or if only one group activity was observed and children were intentionally pulled out of the classroom for one-to-one therapy.

3.1 Score YES if all children participate in at least one daily group activity with their peers (other than snack time) during the day. If a child is intentionally pulled out of a group activity to participate in a different group or one-to-one activity in the classroom (e.g., small-group intervention with two to three children, one-to-one activity with a teacher), then you may still score YES if the activity was intentionally planned to meet individual learning goals. You can interview the teacher in such cases. Ask, "Do children participate in daily planned group activities?" Continue your question to find out more about the purpose and intention to remove a child from a whole-group activity. Do not give credit if children are removed from group activities and allowed to wander around in the classroom as a result of adults' lack of effort to support children's engagement during group activities.

3.2 If at least one child is not engaged for the majority of the time, and no efforts were made to support participation, then do not give credit.

5.1 Score YES if you observe several examples used with the majority of children to support active and sustained participation in the activity. Adaptations can be made in the 1) materials, physical space, and equipment (e.g., use of visual props, adaptive equipment, thicker brush); 2) objectives, structure, and grouping (e.g., while other children are drawing shapes, one child's goal is to trace a circle); or 3) instructional support (e.g., offering hand-over-hand assistance, modeling for child how to perform an activity, adapting directions and prompts, repeating instructions). This indicator does not assess how groups are formed. Observe groups, including groups only of children with disabilities). You can also score YES if no adaptations were observed and all children with disabilities seemed actively engaged for 85% or more of the activity time. If a child had to be removed from a group activity for behavior support or joined a different small group or one-to-one activity/intervention in the classroom, then consider the previous examples of strategies for supporting engagement.

5.2 Score YES if the majority of the children under observation and the majority of the rest of the group are actively engaged most of the time.

7.1 Score YES if children with disabilities are actively engaged and adults are available to provide individualized support for every child, if needed. Also, score YES if a child has difficulty participating in the group, but adults consistently use strategies to support his or her needs (e.g., child runs away during group activity and adult gradually uses more explicit verbal and physical prompts to encourage child participation). Score NO if at least one child has difficulty participating in a group activity and adults do not consistently accommodate his or her needs to facilitate participation.

NOTES _____

_____

_____

_____

_____

_____

_____

Figure 2.9. *(continued)*

How Is Assessment Information Gathered?

- Observation
- Interview

What Does It Look Like in a High-Quality Inclusive Classroom?

Kelly works together with her co-teacher to adjust group activities as needed to encourage participation of all children in the group. For example, during a small-group art activity in which children were using paintbrushes to paint leaves they collected outdoors, Kelly provided hand-over-hand assistance for Louisa, a child with a fine motor coordination difficulty, to fingerpaint her leaves. The second part of the activity involved cutting through paper to form different shapes, and Louisa worked on one of her individualized goals that involved sorting out different shapes alongside her peers.

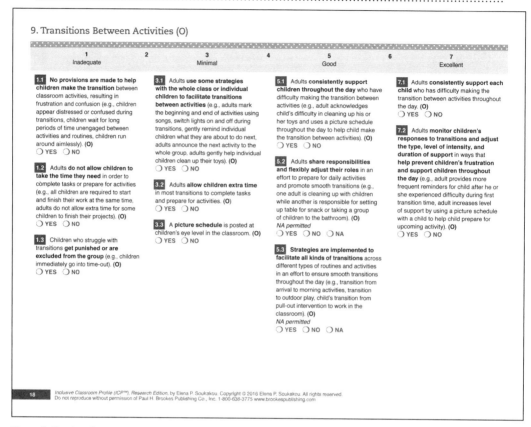

Figure 2.10. Item 9

ITEM 9: Transitions Between Activities

Item 9 (see Figure 2.10) assesses the quality of provisions and strategies for promoting smooth transitions between activities and supporting children who experience difficulty during transitions.

What Does This Item Assess?

- Classroom provisions for promoting smooth transitions between activities and classroom routines

- Adult use of individualized support for children experiencing difficulty making the transition between activities and routines

- Adult use of visual supports to facilitate transitions

- Teaming and collaboration between adults for planning for and facilitating transitions between activities and routines

Criteria for Rating Indicators

Item 9 assesses the quality of provisions and strategies for promoting smooth transitions between activities and supporting children who experience difficulty during transitions.

3.1   Programs may use different strategies depending on their philosophy, which may not include strategies with the whole group (e.g., using transition music or loud sound at the beginning and end of transitions). Score YES if at least one strategy was observed to facilitate smooth transitions, such as adults gently approaching individual children reminding them it is time to prepare for an upcoming activity. Credit can be given if the strategy was observed with some but not all of the children under observation (e.g., teacher gently reminded some children about upcoming activity but not all of the children under observation). Yet, if you observe at least one child demonstrating difficulty making a transition (e.g., child seems confused and frustrated during transition), and no efforts were observed to support his or her transition, then do not give credit for this indicator.

3.2   You can give credit if children were able to make the transition between activities without needing extra time.

5.1   Score YES if the majority of children who show difficulty with transitions are supported most of the time.

5.2   NA is permitted if there is only one teacher in the classroom during the day of the observation.

5.3   NA is permitted if only one transition was observed (e.g., from morning circle time to free-choice activity and playtime).

7.1   Score YES if teachers use individualized strategies in a consistent manner throughout the day for each child who demonstrates difficulty making the transition.

NOTES _____

_____

_____

_____

_____

_____

_____

Figure 2.10.   *(continued)*

How Is Assessment Information Gathered?

- Observation

What Does It Look Like in a High-Quality Inclusive Classroom?

Adults in Kelly's classroom share responsibilities and flexibly adjust their roles in an effort to prepare for daily activities and promote smooth transitions. Adults plan activities and supports for the whole group in an effort to ensure smooth transitions. Adults use specific, individualized strategies for children who experience greater difficulty making the transition between activities. For example, Kelly uses a soft musical tune to signal the end of transitions with the whole group. Sam, however, requires additional support to transition between activities. Kelly and her co-teacher created a picture schedule, and she goes through the picture schedule with Sam, who finds it very helpful to look at the visual symbols of upcoming activities, prior to the end of each routine.

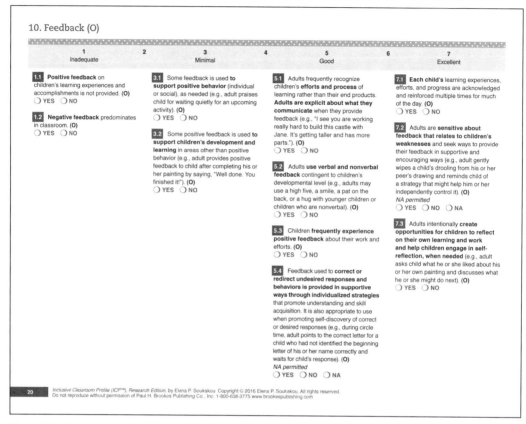

Figure 2.11.   Item 10

ITEM 10: Feedback

Item 10 (see Figure 2.11) measures the nature, frequency, and type of feedback that is offered to support children's positive behavior, efforts, learning, and development.

What Does This Item Assess?

- Adults provide children positive feedback on their efforts, behaviors, and learning

- Adults use different types of feedback (e.g., corrective feedback, positive reinforcement) to support important goals (e.g., positive behavior, learning, engagement)

- Adults use process-oriented feedback

- Adults use verbal and nonverbal feedback

- Adults provide sensitive feedback in responsive and supportive ways

Criteria for Rating Indicators

Item 10 measures the nature, frequency, and type of feedback that is offered to support children's positive behavior, efforts, learning, and development.

1.1   Score YES if this is true for the majority of children observed.

3.2   Feedback on children's development and learning may include constructive comments related to how children think, engage in activities and interactions, use materials, and approach various tasks. Examples include praising a child for completing his or her activity; complimenting a child for his or her persistence in solving a puzzle; commenting to two children about the way they are working together on a project. Several examples need to be observed with different children.

5.1   Process-oriented feedback focuses on children's efforts and process of doing things rather than their end products. Adult feedback goes beyond telegraphic statements to descriptions of what they are commenting about. Score YES if the majority of the feedback observed during the assessment period was effort based. Many examples across different children throughout the day need to be observed.

5.2   You may still give credit if only verbal feedback was observed in a classroom if all the children under observation seemed capable of understanding the verbal feedback presented to them.

5.3   The number of examples might depend on the number of children, but, as a general rule, score YES if many examples of positive feedback are observed across the majority of the children and examples of positive feedback are observed across different contexts or activities.

5.4   This indicator is rated when adults are observed providing feedback that aims at correcting, or redirecting children's responses, behaviors, and actions related to their learning, engagement in activities, and social interactions. Score YES if corrective feedback is provided in supportive ways for the majority of the children most of the time. Feedback is focused on the desired responses/behaviors (e.g., adult avoids simply stating what children did or did not do appropriately), involves the use of individual scaffolding strategies (e.g., adult asks children to trace a circle in the sand, and upon an incorrect attempt from a child, adult models how to trace the correct shape for the child), and is provided in ways that encourage self-discovery of alternative responses (e.g., adult uses nonverbal prompting and wait time for child to help him or her identify an animal in a picture book by saying, "I think I can see a yellow duckling swimming in the lake," while pointing on the relevant part of the page to help the child identify the animal). NA is permitted if there were no opportunities to observe this type of feedback during the observation period.

7.2   Do not give credit if you observe at least one instance in which feedback that relates to children's sensitive weaknesses is provided to any child in the classroom in nonsupportive ways. NA is permitted if no examples of such feedback were observed with the children under observation.

7.3   This indicator can be scored based on one or more examples observed with any child (with or without disabilities) in the classroom. Credit may also be given when such feedback is provided to a group of children (e.g., adult encourages children during circle time to reflect on a group project).

NOTES

Figure 2.11.   *(continued)*

How Is Assessment Information Gathered?

- Observation

What Does It Look Like in a High-Quality Inclusive Classroom?

Kelly uses different forms of feedback in her classroom to support children's learning and development. Adults frequently use feedback that focuses on children's efforts and process of doing things rather than solely on their end products. Adults also use nonverbal feedback when needed, such as high fives, a pat on the back, positive gestures, and facial expressions. Adults who provide corrective feedback use specific strategies in supportive ways to promote understanding. For example, Kelly observed Chris, a 3-year-old boy with a developmental delay, working hard to solve a number puzzle during free playtime. Kelly asked him how he was trying to figure out how to put the pieces together. When Chris explained his strategy, Kelly said, "I can see you are working very hard and your strategy seems very helpful." Kelly invited Chris to reflect on his earlier work and invited him to share his strategy with his peers during circle time.

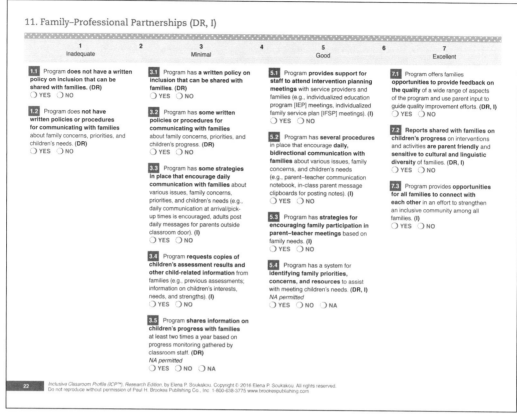

Figure 2.12. Item 11

ITEM 11: Family–Professional Partnerships

Item 11 (see Figure 2.12) measures the policies and procedures implemented to encourage and foster partnerships between the children's setting and the children's families.

What Does This Item Assess?

- Inclusive policies and procedures for communicating with families
- Support for staff to participate in meetings with families to plan for and discuss children's individualized education programs
- Procedures implemented daily for encouraging bidirectional communication with families
- Procedures for sharing and exchanging information on children's progress
- Opportunities for families to contribute information on family priorities
- Opportunities for families to provide feedback on the quality of the program

How Is Assessment Information Gathered?

- Interview
- Documentation review

Criteria for Rating Indicators

Item 11 measures the policies and procedures implemented to encourage and foster partnerships between the children's setting and their families. Indicators 1.1, 1.2, 3.1, and 3.2 can be scored based on documentation provided by any staff member of the program. If the teacher is not aware of existing policies, then you may ask to speak to the program director or other program staff. All other information should be provided by program staff who teach in the classroom. Documentation needs to be provided and reviewed for all indicators marked with (DR).

1.1 & 3.1 Ask, "Do you have a written policy on inclusion that can be shared with families?" A written policy on inclusion might be displayed at the program, be available on request, or be found on the program's web site.

1.2 & 3.2 Ask, "Do you have any written policies/procedures for communicating with families?" Policies, guidelines, and procedures can be found in policy documents, online brochures, parent handbooks, program leaflets, and similar resources. Written policies/procedures should relate specifically to communication with families rather than generally about families' rights and involvement.

3.3 Ask, "Do you have any procedures for regularly communicating with families about daily issues, family concerns, priorities, resources, and children's needs?" Score YES if program staff report at least one example in place for encouraging daily communication with families (e.g., informal conversations during arrival/departure times, e-mail, weekly log).

3.4 Ask, "Do you request copies of children's assessments and any other child-related information from families, such as information on children's interests, strengths, and learning needs? What other child-related information might you request from families?" Score YES if program staff report that they request copies of assessments and some additional child-related information.

3.5 Ask, "How do you share information on children's progress with families? What kind of child progress monitoring information do you exchange with families?" Score YES if documentation evidence of child progress monitoring assessment data is available to share with families (e.g., child progress report, summary assessment results for individual child, recently recorded assessment scores). NA is permitted if an ICP assessment is conducted in the first 2 months of a school year and, therefore, program cannot provide available documentation.

5.1 Ask, "Are you or other staff available to attend intervention planning meetings such as IEP or IFSP meetings with service providers and families?" Score YES if program staff report that they are available to participate in intervention planning meetings.

5.2 Ask, "Do you have any procedures for regularly communicating with families about daily issues, family concerns, priorities, resources, and children's needs?" Score YES if program staff describe at least two examples that enable both classroom staff and families to communicate with each other about various daily issues (bidirectional communication). Examples should describe procedures other than informal conversations during pick-up/arrival times (e.g., parent–teacher communication notebook, e-mail/web mail, in-class parent–teacher communication box for exchanging messages).

5.3 Ask, "How do you encourage family participation in parent–teacher meetings?" Score YES if program staff provide at least two examples describing how they actively encourage families to participate in parent–teacher meetings. Examples might include sending family-friendly reminder invitation letters/e-mails to families, regularly updating information on the content and benefits of parent–teacher meetings on the program's web site, and contacting individual families by telephone/e-mail to encourage participation.

5.4 Ask, "Do you have a system for identifying family priorities, concerns, and resources?" Score YES if program shares documentation evidence of a written system (e.g., checklist, questionnaire) for identifying family concerns, priorities, and resources. Program staff also report that it is used at least twice a year.

7.1 Ask, "Do you offer all families opportunities to provide feedback on the quality of a wide range of aspects of the program?" Score YES if program provides documentation evidence of a written system for enabling families to offer their feedback.

7.3 Ask, "Do you provide all families with opportunities to connect with other families from your program or your community? How might you do this?" Score YES if program staff report several examples of ways in which they help families connect with other families. Examples might include organizing family day/evening events at the program site, providing information on local family support groups, and designating a parent as a leader/coordinator of family meetings and events for the program.

Figure 2.12. *(continued)*

What Does It Look Like in a High-Quality Inclusive Classroom?

Kelly's program has a written policy on inclusion and specific procedures for communicating with families about family concerns, priorities, and children's progress. Several practices that encourage daily, bidirectional communication with families are included in those procedures. For example, each child/family has a daily communication book in which families and teachers can exchange daily messages, including private notes. Kelly also uses e-mail daily to communicate with families. At the end of each day, classroom staff post messages about the day's activities and children's experiences on a white board outside the classroom to share with families. Kelly's program also provides support for staff to attend intervention planning meetings with service providers and families. To exchange information on children's progress with families, the program actively encourages families to participate regularly in progress meetings and shares reports of children's progress that are parent friendly and sensitive to the cultural and linguistic diversity of families. Kelly's program also uses a system for identifying family priorities, concerns, and resources to assist with meeting children's needs. This year, Kelly's program started using a system for receiving regular feedback from families about the quality of the program and their experiences.

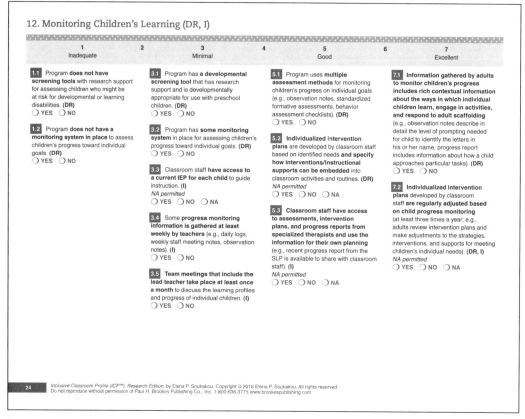

Figure 2.13.   Item 12

ITEM 12: Monitoring Children's Learning

Item 12 (see Figure 2.13) assesses the quality of procedures in place and implemented practices for monitoring children's learning toward individualized goals.

What Does This Item Assess?

- Assessment systems and methods for monitoring children's progress toward individual goals
- Frequency of use of progress monitoring systems
- Quality of intervention planning methods
- Use of progress monitoring data to adjust interventions and instruction
- Evidence that planning includes interventions that support children's needs in their home and community

How Is Assessment Information Gathered?

- Interview
- Documentation review

Criteria for Rating Indicators

Item 12 assesses the quality of procedures in place and implemented practices for monitoring children's learning toward individualized goals. Documentation needs to be provided and reviewed for all indicators marked with (DR).

1.1 Ask, " Do you have a way for identifying a child who might be at risk for developmental delay or a learning disability?" Documentation evidence of a standardized screening tool with research support is needed.

1.2 Ask, "How do you monitor children's progress on various learning and developmental goals?" Score YES if no documentation evidence of any kind of progress monitoring system is in place for assessing children's progress. Examples include standardized assessment tools, daily log indicating children's progress, teacher-developed checklists, and observation notes. Examples of children's work or photographs do not count as an example for this indicator.

3.1 Ask, " Do you have a way for identifying a child who might be at risk for developmental delay or a learning disability?" Documentation evidence of a standardized screening tool with research support is needed.

3.2 Ask, "How do you monitor children's progress on various learning and developmental goals?" Score YES if at least one method is used to monitor children's progress, (e.g., observation sticky notes, general anecdotal records, curriculum-based assessment). Examples of children's work or photographs do not count as an example for this indicator.

3.4 Ask, "How often do you monitor children's progress on various goals?" Score YES if teacher reports that some information on children's progress is collected at least weekly.

3.5 Ask, "How often do staff meetings take place with a goal to discuss children's profiles?" Score YES if teacher reports that team meetings take place at least monthly.

5.1 Ask, "How do you monitor children's progress on various learning and developmental goals?" Score YES if there is documentation evidence of at least two methods (one informal and one formal) for monitoring children's progress. Observation sticky notes, anecdotal records, and daily log are examples of authentic, informal assessment methods. Standardized formative assessment measures and research-based developmental assessments are examples of formal, standardized assessment methods. This indicator assesses how adults monitor children's progress throughout the term. Therefore, do not consider end-of-year reports.

5.2 Ask, "Do you have an individualized intervention plan for each child with a disability that describes a child's current needs as well as the specific interventions/instructional

supports that are being implemented?" Individual intervention plans can take different forms and can be developed by classroom staff or jointly with specialists working with children. Intervention plans describe how specific interventions, strategies (e.g., a targeted behavior intervention, a structured language intervention), and resources (e.g., visual communication system) are implemented in the classroom to support a child's learning needs. An example of a plan needs to be provided describing areas of need and the relevant instructional strategies, interventions, and supports that are being/will be implemented to support a child's needs. NA is permitted if the ICP assessment is being conducted at the beginning of a year (e.g., first 6–8 weeks), a child is undergoing an evaluation process at the time of the ICP assessment, or an intervention plan is in the process of being developed.

5.3 Ask, "Do you have access to assessments, intervention plans, and progress reports from specialized therapists? How do you use such information?" Score YES if teacher reports that classroom staff have access to such information and use it to plan and adjust classroom instruction. NA is permitted if children are not receiving any therapy/specialist services at the time of the ICP assessment.

7.1 Score YES if documentation evidence from one or more sources of progress monitoring data gathered by classroom staff (e.g., observation notes) shows that adults gather contextualized information on children's individual learning profiles. Such information can be included in weekly observation notes, daily logs, quarterly progress reports, and other progress monitoring methods (e.g., observation sticky notes describe how a child responded to multiple-step directions and the type and level of support he or she needed to follow directions). Progress monitoring data might also describe the contexts in which interventions take place or the contexts in which children engage in activities (e.g., adults document information on when, where, and with whom children approach different tasks, try new things, and practice their skills).

7.2 Ask, "How often do you review and adjust intervention plans for individual children?" Score YES if teacher reports that intervention plans are reviewed and adjusted at least three times a year for each child. Documentation also needs to be provided showing an example of an intervention plan for an individual child that was revised or adjusted. Examples of intervention plans need to clearly indicate instructional adjustments (if needed) in a) children's individual goals, b) strategies/interventions for supporting children's needs, and c) adult(s) responsible for implementing strategies. NA is permitted if an ICP assessment is being conducted in the beginning of a year (e.g., first 6–8 weeks), a child is undergoing an evaluation process at the time of the ICP assessment, or an intervention plan is in the process of being developed.

Figure 2.13. *(continued)*

What Does It Look Like in a High-Quality Inclusive Classroom?

Kelly's program uses multiple assessment methods for monitoring children's progress on individual goals. They use a combination of research-based formative assessment tools, observation notes, behavioral assessment checklists, and various other teacher-made assessment tools. An individualized intervention plan for each child is developed by classroom staff based on identified needs and specifies how interventions and instructional supports can be embedded into classroom activities. All classroom staff have access to assessments, intervention plans, and progress reports from specialized therapists, and they use information for their own planning. Kelly gathers assessment information to monitor children's progress on a weekly basis and uses the information she gathers to review intervention plans and make any needed adjustments to the strategies, interventions, and supports for each child. For example, Kelly was keeping a running record of Maya's participation during storytime to monitor her engagement following a recent embedded activity they had started implementing a few weeks ago to support her understanding of story facts. In her notes, Kelly recorded that Maya found it helpful to use story props to act out the story prior to and during retelling a story. She also noted that Maya might need more frequent prompting by an adult to help her connect the events of a story.

3

Administration of the ICP

Administration of the ICP involves direct observation of the physical environment, daily routines, and activities both inside and outside of the classroom. A few items require a short teacher interview and documentation review. An ICP assessment needs to be conducted by an external observer and should be scheduled during regular classroom routines and at times when all children, including those with disabilities, are present.

OBSERVATION FOCUS

Conducting an ICP assessment entails observing all children with identified disabilities in the classroom. Scores on each item represent the quality of observed practices implemented to support the active participation of children with disabilities in the classroom. Assessors also observe all adults in the room who interact with the children under observation, giving a score that best represents the quality of provisions and practices that were implemented with the children. Many of the ICP items also require observation of the physical space, materials, and equipment that are used in the classroom. Because the focus of the ICP is on practices that support high-quality inclusion, practices are always observed in the context of peer interactions, activities, and daily routines that take place with all children in the classroom.

PLACE AND DURATION OF ASSESSMENT

An ICP assessment requires 2 ½–3 hours of classroom observation. An interview and documentation review complete the assessment and will require about 20 minutes of additional time. An ICP assessment typically takes place in a morning or afternoon session. An appropriate assessment requires that observations take place in all contexts used by adults to support children's learning and development, including indoor and outdoor space, rooms where small-group interventions and activities take place, areas for snack time, and the children's bathrooms. It is possible to conduct an assessment that bridges a morning and an afternoon session. To rate the ICP items appropriately, assessors should ensure that the assessment time includes observation of classroom practices and social interactions as they take place across a variety of learning contexts, including children's free-choice time in centers, adult-guided whole-group and small-group activities (e.g., storytime), and transitions between activities and routines.

PREPARING FOR AN ICP ASSESSMENT

Before administering the rating scale, observers should be familiar with the scale's items, administration, and scoring procedures. Assessors who are planning an ICP classroom visit should inform program staff ahead of time about the need to conduct a short teacher interview and documentation review. The teacher interview and documentation review should be scheduled at a time when adults are not interacting with children or supervising classroom activities.

THE CLASSROOM OBSERVATION

Before starting the assessment, assessors will need to ask the lead teacher to point out the child or children with identified disabilities who will be observed. During the observation period, assessors place themselves at an area in the classroom where they can clearly observe the classroom routines and social interactions that take place. Observers are encouraged to conduct a nonparticipant observation to ensure valid and reliable assessment, and, therefore, interactions with children ought to be minimized.

Assessors who are observing more than one child need to intentionally observe each child's experiences across different learning contexts and interactions with adults and peers. Observers are encouraged to take notes on each child in the form of a running record to assist with their ratings. Once the ICP assessment is completed, observers can reflect on their observation notes to rate individual items and apply the scoring criteria that are listed under each item. Observation notes can be recorded in a notebook or directly on the ICP rating scale form.

Users of the ICP might also want to gather additional information about the classroom before conducting the observation, including the number of adults that will be present in the classroom during the assessment, whether any of the children will be receiving any specific interventions, or whether any of the children will be receiving in-class supports from therapists (e.g., speech-language pathologist) or other professionals (e.g., hearing specialist). Such contextual information might assist users of the ICP, such as professional development providers, early childhood educators, and program administrators, to reflect on assessment results and guide professional development activities for improving classroom practice.

THE INTERVIEW AND DOCUMENTATION REVIEW

The interview and documentation review needs to be conducted with the lead teacher at a time when he or she is not supervising children's activities. It is recommended that observers inform the lead teacher ahead of time about the need to ask a few questions about the observation as well as to review certain documents. Observers ask a set of specific, structured questions that relate to specific quality indicators. These questions can be found for each item on the accompanying page labeled Criteria for Rating Indicators as well as on the Interview Summary Sheet following the last item on the ICP. Items and indicators that are scored based on observation are marked on the item page with the symbols to indicate *observation* (O), *interview* (I), or *documentation review* (DR). Observers are guided by the (I) and (DR) symbols on the item pages to identify which indicators require an interview or documentation review and the related questions under each item's Criteria for Rating Indicators section. Assessors need to ask the questions as stated on the ICP rating scale and rate teachers' responses by following the relevant criteria for rating indicators.

Similarly, the documentation review requires looking over certain documents, including inclusive policies, procedures, and systems for assessing and monitoring children's progress. Programs are not required to submit any documentation prior to the ICP classroom visit. Assessors are encouraged, however, to inform the program about the need to review certain documents on the day of the assessment in order to factor in the lead teacher's availability and the time needed for providing the necessary documents as part of the interview process. The main documents to be reviewed include 1) the program's inclusive policy, 2) child developmental screening and progress monitoring assessments used by the program, 3) procedures for communicating with families, and 4) individual child intervention plans.

TRAINING

It is recommended that users receive training from certified/approved trainers prior to using the measure and applying the scoring guidelines. The ICP training program supports users in accurately and reliably administering and scoring the measure. Accuracy in administration and scoring is achieved by learning how to administer and apply the scoring procedures consistent with the ICP guidelines. For example, the ICP training program supports users in conducting a classroom observation using the ICP tool, as well as planning for and conducting the interview and documentation review. Reliability training is another component of the ICP training program designed to support users in applying the scoring criteria consistent with the ICP scoring standards. This part of the training involves conducting reliability observations in classrooms alongside an ICP trainer. This process is followed by face-to-face debriefing sessions in which ICP users compare and discuss their observations and ratings with their trainer and are supported in applying the scoring criteria and reaching satisfactory interobserver agreement. For information on ICP training, contact Paul H. Brookes Publishing Co. at seminars@brookespublishing.com.

4

Scoring the ICP

This section provides information on scoring the ICP items. Users of the ICP are strongly encouraged to follow the general and specific scoring guidelines for rating the ICP indicators and items. Adhering to the steps and considerations provided in this manual will ensure that users are interpreting and scoring the data gathered through observation, interview, and documentation review with accuracy and reliability.

GENERAL SCORING GUIDELINES

Each ICP item is rated on a Likert-type scale of 1 (inadequate) to 7 (excellent). Scores for each item are given based on the following guidelines. The symbols for *observation* (O), *interview* (I), and *documentation review* (DR) are next to the items and indicators, and are used to guide the observer on how to collect the necessary information. To score each one of the ICP items, the assessor reads each qualitative indicator listed under each column and marks it with a YES if the classroom practice/indicator was manifested during the assessment period or a NO if the classroom practice/indicator was not manifested during the assessment. A separate page next to each item page includes a list of specific criteria that need to be considered for rating the item's quality indicators. After rating all qualitative indicators within an item with a YES, NO, or not applicable (NA), the item can be scored according to the following instructions:

- A rating of 1 is given if any one indicator under column 1 is scored YES.

- A rating of 2 is given when all indicators under column 1 are scored NO and at least half of the indicators under column 3 are scored YES.

- A rating of 3 is given when all indicators under column 1 are scored NO and all indicators under column 3 are scored YES.

- A rating of 4 is given when all indicators under column 3 are met and at least half of the indicators under column 5 are scored YES.

- A rating of 5 is given when all indicators under column 5 are met.

- A rating of 6 is given when all indicators under column 5 are scored YES and at least half of the indicators under column 7 are scored YES.

- A rating of 7 is given when all indicators under column 7 are met.

- A score of NA permitted: Not Applicable is given when indicated. Indicators assessed NA permitted are not counted when determining the rating for an item.

A total score for the ICP rating scale is computed by taking the average of the individual item ratings once each item on the scale is given a score from 1 to 7. Ratings for individual indicators and items, as well as the ICP composite score, can be recorded on the ICP Score Sheet.

THE ICP SCORE SHEET

The ICP Score Sheet (Figure 4.1) can be found at the end of the ICP rating scale. Ratings can be recorded on the ICP Score Sheet during or following a classroom observation.

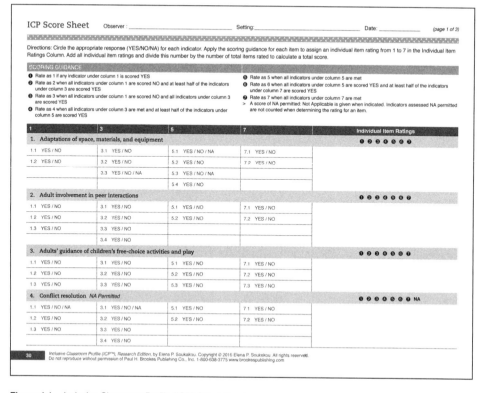

Figure 4.1. Inclusive Classroom Profile (ICP) Score Sheet.

ICP Score Sheet

(page 2 of 3)

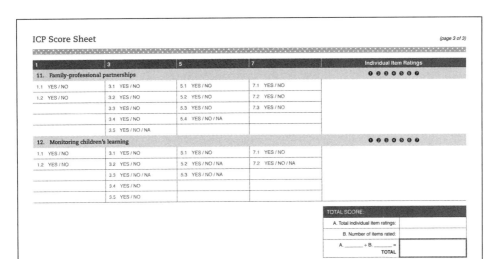

1	3	5	7	Individual Item Ratings
5. Membership				① ② ③ ④ ⑤ ⑥ ⑦
1.1 YES / NO / NA	3.1 YES / NO / NA	5.1 YES / NO	7.1 YES / NO	
1.2 YES / NO	3.2 YES / NO / NA	5.2 YES / NO / NA	7.2 YES / NO	
1.3 YES / NO	3.3 YES / NO	5.3 YES / NO		
	3.4 YES / NO / NA			
6. Relationships between adults and children				① ② ③ ④ ⑤ ⑥ ⑦
1.1 YES / NO	3.1 YES / NO	5.1 YES / NO	7.1 YES / NO	
1.2 YES / NO	3.2 YES / NO	5.2 YES / NO	7.2 YES / NO / NA	
1.3 YES / NO	3.3 YES / NO	5.3 YES / NO	7.3 YES / NO	
7. Support for communication				① ② ③ ④ ⑤ ⑥ ⑦
1.1 YES / NO	3.1 YES / NO	5.1 YES / NO	7.1 YES / NO	
1.2 YES / NO	3.2 YES / NO	5.2 YES / NO	7.2 YES / NO	
	3.3 YES / NO	5.3 YES / NO		
8. Adaptations of group activities *NA Permitted*				① ② ③ ④ ⑤ ⑥ ⑦ NA
1.1 YES / NO	3.1 YES / NO	5.1 YES / NO	7.1 YES / NO	
1.2 YES / NO	3.2 YES / NO	5.2 YES / NO	7.2 YES / NO	
	3.3 YES / NO			
9. Transitions between activities				① ② ③ ④ ⑤ ⑥ ⑦
1.1 YES / NO	3.1 YES / NO	5.1 YES / NO	7.1 YES / NO	
1.2 YES / NO	3.2 YES / NO	5.2 YES / NO / NA	7.2 YES / NO	
1.3 YES / NO	3.3 YES / NO	5.3 YES / NO / NA		
10. Feedback				① ② ③ ④ ⑤ ⑥ ⑦
1.1 YES / NO	3.1 YES / NO	5.1 YES / NO	7.1 YES / NO	
1.2 YES / NO	3.2 YES / NO	5.2 YES / NO	7.2 YES / NO / NA	
		5.3 YES / NO	7.3 YES / NO	
		5.4 YES / NO / NA		

ICP Score Sheet

(page 3 of 3)

1	3	5	7	Individual Item Ratings
11. Family-professional partnerships				① ② ③ ④ ⑤ ⑥ ⑦
1.1 YES / NO	3.1 YES / NO	5.1 YES / NO	7.1 YES / NO	
1.2 YES / NO	3.2 YES / NO	5.2 YES / NO	7.2 YES / NO	
	3.3 YES / NO	5.3 YES / NO	7.3 YES / NO	
	3.4 YES / NO	5.4 YES / NO / NA		
	3.5 YES / NO / NA			
12. Monitoring children's learning				① ② ③ ④ ⑤ ⑥ ⑦
1.1 YES / NO	3.1 YES / NO	5.1 YES / NO	7.1 YES / NO	
1.2 YES / NO	3.2 YES / NO	5.2 YES / NO / NA	7.2 YES / NO / NA	
	3.3 YES / NO / NA	5.3 YES / NO / NA		
	3.4 YES / NO			
	3.5 YES / NO			

TOTAL SCORE:	
A. Total individual item ratings:	
B. Number of items rated:	
A. _____ ÷ B. _____ = **TOTAL**	

....

   Assessors need to adhere to the following steps to calculate and record a total ICP score profile:

1. For each item listed on the score sheet, provide a score for each indicator by circling the appropriate response (YES, NO, NA).

2. After scoring all indicators for an item, apply the general scoring guidelines for each item to come up with a rating from 1 to 7 and circle your rating on the space provided next to the item. You will be able to review the ratings provided for each of the 12 ICP items at the end of this step.

3. To calculate a total score, add all individual item ratings (ranging from 1 to 7) and divide this number by the number of items that were rated as part of your ICP assessment. You can then enter the total score in the box provided at the end of the score sheet. For example, if you scored only 11 out of the 12 ICP items, then you will need to divide the added ratings of the ICP items by 11 to create a total score.

SPECIFIC SCORING CONSIDERATIONS

The first important step in learning how to score the ICP items is reviewing the general scoring guidelines. The second step involves reviewing specific scoring considerations, such as criteria for rating indicators, dimensions rated by the scoring criteria, as well as considerations related to the focus of the observation.

Criteria for Rating Indicators

Each ICP item is accompanied by a set of criteria for rating the quality indicators of that particular item. The criteria are designed to help assessors rate items accurately and consistently. The criteria can be found on the page labeled Criteria for Rating Indicators that accompanies each ICP item page. The section that lists the criteria for rating the indicators of a particular item includes a brief description of the item and provides any specific administration issues that need to be considered. It is important to note that criteria are not listed for each quality indicator, only for those that require additional clarification. To apply the scoring criteria for each item, assessors need to look for the corresponding indicator marked with a number on the left-hand side of each listed criterion (e.g., 5.2) and consider the criterion or criteria for that indicator. The listed criteria typically serve the following purpose: 1) provide the guidelines for scoring various or special cases with a YES or NO; 2) define and operationalize key concepts and terms; and 3) provide examples of behaviors, strategies, and resources to help assessors rate the indicators.

Dimensions Rated by the Scoring Criteria

The ICP items rate a wide range of practices within the 12 domains of classroom quality. The quality of implementation is assessed across a 7-point scale by evaluating the following key dimensions of quality: 1) occurrence of a particular practice or components of a particular practice (e.g., Is there a system in place for monitoring children's progress? Does progress monitoring involve the use of authentic and research-based formative assessment tools?), 2) frequency (e.g., Do children have many opportunities in the day to make choices?),

3) consistency (e.g., Are children consistently supported throughout the day to make the transition between activities when needed?), and 4) individualization (e.g., Was each child engaged during whole-group activities?). Matching practices with appropriate dimensions for assessment is a key process in measurement design (Viswanathan, 2005). For example, frequency might be a more meaningful and appropriate dimension to assess in some practices than in others.

Children as the Focus of Observation

During an ICP observation, assessors may observe one or more children, depending on how many children have been identified by the teacher as having a disability. Assessors who are observing more than one child need to ensure equal observation time for each child during activities and interactions because these are related to the indicators under assessment. This does not require a time sampling observation schedule. It can be achieved by being familiar with the scale items and observing intentionally so that each child's experience has a chance to be observed in relation to the practices being assessed. The criteria for rating indicators provide additional specific guidelines for rating indicators when more than one child is being observed.

- When two children are being observed, the term *majority* requires that the assessed practice needs to be observed with both children (unless specified different in the criteria for rating a particular indicator).

- When more than two children are being observed, the term *majority* requires that the practice under assessment needs to be observed with more than half of the children (unless specified different in the criteria for rating a particular indicator).

Start and End of Observation

- An ICP assessment starts when all children to be observed are present in the classroom and assessors have identified the children to be observed.

- When a child arrives late or leaves before the end of the assessment, assessors can continue with the observation and consider those children's experiences as part of their assessment. In such cases, assessment of concepts such as the majority of time will need to be based on the total time that each child was involved in the practice under assessment. For example, if a child arrived in the middle of free-play time, and an indicator required assessing the extent to which a practice was observed for the majority of time, then the assessor would need to consider the total time that the child participated in free-play time and rate the indicator based on the majority of that time period.

Adults as the Focus of Observation

When an indicator requires the observation of adults, consider the particular practice under assessment, the quality of support provided to the children, and whether the support was provided/needed across contexts. If a majority of adults or all adults need to be considered for scoring a particular indicator, then this is stated in the indicator and in the related criteria for scoring indicators. In cases in which the majority of adults is required for rating a particular indicator, and two adults were present in the classroom, then the assessed practice needs to be observed with both adults.

INTERPRETING AND SHARING
RATINGS FROM AN ICP ASSESSMENT

An ICP total score can take any rating between 1 and 7. To interpret a total score on the 7-point scale, assessors need to map an obtained total score on the equivalent level of quality (1 = inadequate, 7 = excellent). For example, a total score of 4.7 would reflect a classroom that meets all the basic requirements and demonstrates emerging practices of higher quality (e.g., practices at a good quality level). Assessors conducting an ICP assessment can calculate the total score as well as report item scores separately. Once an ICP assessment is completed and all ratings have been recorded, assessors can share assessment information with program staff as part of a quality improvement program by linking assessment data with instructional decision making.

Frequently Asked Questions

1. **Who can use the ICP measure?**

    The ICP measure can be used by early childhood teachers, professional development providers, researchers, and other practitioners who are familiar with the field of early childhood inclusion.

2. **Is training needed to use the ICP?**

    Yes. Training is strongly recommended in order to use the ICP in a reliable and accurate way. The current training program includes a face-to-face overview of the ICP administration and scoring procedures and three to four live classroom observations with an ICP qualified trainer to help users meet reliability proficiency.

3. **Where can I gain access to the training?**

    For information on ICP training, contact Paul H. Brookes Publishing Co. at seminars@brookespublishing.com

4. **In what type of early childhood settings can the ICP be used?**

    The ICP can be used in various inclusive early childhood programs (serving children 2–5 years of age), including child care centers, public preschool, private programs, and playgroups. According to the definition used in the ICP measure, *inclusive* refers to programs that include at least one child with an identified special education need.

5. **Can the ICP be used in classrooms serving children younger and/or older than the recommended age group?**

    The ICP has been designed and field-tested for use in classrooms serving children 2–5 years of age. Further research is needed to test the extent to which the ICP tool can be used in classrooms serving younger or older children.

6. **Who can interpret the ICP scores after an ICP assessment?**

    Any user who has received training by the author or a certified ICP trainer will be able to interpret the ratings from an ICP assessment.

7. **Can the ICP assessment be conducted at the same time as other program quality assessments?**

Assessors conducting an ICP assessment need to focus exclusively on their observation, interview, and documentation review in the time frame recommended by the ICP administration guidelines. Therefore, an ICP assessment can be conducted on the same day and at the same time with other classroom quality instruments, provided that a separate assessor would be conducting a different assessment.

8. **Can I give credit to higher quality indicators if lower quality indicators are scored *no*?**

The ICP measurement system requires a score to be given at each item based on quality indicators that are scored *yes* and *no* under each column. This means that even if certain higher quality indicators are true for that classroom, indicators scored at a lower level determine the score for the item. It might be useful, however, to score all quality indicators of an item if you are using the measure for quality improvement. In such circumstances, information from additional quality indicators might be helpful for programs interested in using assessment data to develop an action plan for improving the quality of inclusive practices.

9. **Can I conduct an ICP assessment over the course of several days?**

An ICP assessment requires 2 ½–3 hours of classroom observation. To complete the assessment, an interview and documentation review will require about 20 minutes of additional time. You need to conduct the whole assessment on the same day within the 3-hour period to obtain reliable and valid assessment information. Many of the quality indicators assess behaviors that are expected to be observed in a 3-hour time period, and, therefore, scoring the quality indicators over several days would weaken the reliability and validity of the ratings.

10. **How much time is needed to conduct the interview? Who can be interviewed?**

To complete an ICP assessment, an interview and documentation review will require about 20 minutes of additional time. It is recommended that users of the ICP inform program staff ahead of time about the need to conduct a short interview and review some documents. The interview needs to be conducted with a lead classroom teacher. This can ensure that information will be gathered by program staff who are familiar with the children participating in the classroom as well as with the routines and practices that are implemented on a daily basis.

11. **How should I rate the ICP items if one or more children identified for observation arrive late or leave the classroom before the end of the observation?**

You can still carry on your observation as planned in cases in which one or more children arrive after your observation has started or leave the classroom before the assessment is complete. The ICP items are designed to measure the quality of practices that were implemented during the observation time, considering the children who were present during that time. Different quality indicators measure different levels of quality, and, therefore, each indicator is accompanied by specific scoring guidelines. The criteria for rating indicators will guide assessors on how to assess various activities, routines, and children's experiences as they occur throughout the observation period. Specific criteria also guide observers when they need to consider the experience of the majority of children present and involved in a particular activity or the experience of individual children.

12. **Can I translate the ICP for use in research or other purposes?**

Information on requesting translation rights can be found at http://www.brookes publishing.com/customer-service/rights-permissions

Translation requests should be sent to rights@brookespublishing.com

References

Arnett, J. (1989). Caregivers in day care centers: Does training matter? *Journal of Applied Developmental Psychology, 10,* 541–552.

Booth, T., & Ainscow, M. (2002). *Index for inclusion: Developing learning and participation in early years and childcare.* Bristol, UK: Centre for Studies on Inclusive Education and East Sussex County Council.

Bredekamp, S., & Copple, C. (Eds.). (1997). *Developmentally appropriate practice in early childhood programs.* Washington, DC: National Association for the Education of Young Children.

Buysse, V. (2011). Access, participation, and supports: The defining features of high-quality inclusion. *Zero to Three, 31,* 24–31.

Buysse, V., & Bailey, D.B. (1993). Behavioral and developmental outcomes in young children with disabilities in integrated and segregated settings: A review of comparative studies. *Journal of Special Education, 26,* 434–461.

Buysse, V., & Hollingsworth, H.L. (2009). Research synthesis points on early childhood inclusion: What every practitioner and all families should know. *Young Exceptional Children, 11,* 18–30.

Buysse, V., Wesley, P.W., Keyes, L., & Bailey, D.B. (1996). Assessing the comfort zone of child care teachers in serving young children with disabilities. *Journal of Early Intervention, 20,* 189–204.

Chang, F., Early, D., & Winton, P. (2005). Early childhood teacher preparation in special education at 2- and 4-year institutions of higher education. *Journal of Early Intervention, 27,* 110–124.

Department for Education and Standards Testing Agency. (2013). *Early years foundation stage program handbook.* Retrieved from https://www.gov.uk/government/uploads/system/uploads/attachment_data/file/249995/Early_years_foundation_stage_profile_handbook_2014.pdf

Division for Early Childhood. (2014). *DEC recommended practices in early intervention/early childhood special education: 2014.* Retrieved from http://www.dec-sped.org/recommendedpractices

Division for Early Childhood/National Association for the Education of Young Children. (2009). *Early childhood inclusion: A joint position statement of the Division for Early Childhood (DEC) and the National Association for the Education of Young Children (NAEYC).* Chapel Hill, NC: University of North Carolina, FPG Child Development Institute.

Early Childhood Outcomes Center. (2005, April). *Family and child outcomes for early intervention and early childhood special education.* Retrieved from http://ectacenter.org/eco/assets/pdfs/ECO_Outcomes_4-13-05.pdf

Early, D., & Winton, P. (2001). Preparing the workforce: Early childhood teacher preparation at 2- and 4-year institutions of higher education. *Early Childhood Research Quarterly, 16,* 285–306.

Harms, T., Clifford, R.M., & Cryer, D. (2005). *Early Childhood Environment Rating Scale-Revised Edition.* New York, NY: Teacher's College Press.

....

Hyson, M., Horm, D.M., & Winton, P.J. (2012). Higher education for early childhood educators and outcomes for young children: Pathways toward greater effectiveness. In R. Pianta, L. Justice, S. Barnett, & S. Sheridan (Eds.), *Handbook of early education* (pp. 553–583). New York, NY: Guilford Press.

Irwin, S.H. (2005). *SpeciaLink child care inclusion practices profile and principles scale.* Winnipeg, Manitoba, Canada: SpeciaLink, The National Centre for Child Care Inclusion.

National Professional Development Center on Inclusion. (2008). *What do we mean by professional development in the early childhood field?* Chapel Hill, NC: University of North Carolina, FPG Child Development Institute.

National Professional Development Center on Inclusion. (2011). *Research synthesis points on quality inclusive practices.* Chapel Hill, NC: University of North Carolina, FPG Child Development Institute.

Odom, S.L., Buysse, V., & Soukakou E. (2011). Inclusion for young children with disabilities: A quarter century of research perspectives. *Journal of Early Intervention, 33,* 344–356

Odom, S.L., Vitztum, J., Wolery, R., Lieber, J., Sandall, S., Hanson, M.J., . . . Horn, E. (2004). Preschool inclusion in the United States: A review of research from an ecological systems perspective. *Journal of Research in Special Educational Needs, 4*(1), 17–49.

Patil, V.H., Singh, S.N., Mishra, S., & Donavan, D.T. (2007). *Parallel analysis engine to aid determining number of factors to retain* [Computer software]. Available from http://smishra.faculty.ku.edu/parallelengine.htm

Pianta, R.C., La Paro, K.M., & Hamre, B.K. (2008). *Classroom Assessment Scoring System® (CLASS®).* Baltimore, MD: Paul H. Brookes Publishing Co.

Sandall, S., Hemmeter, M.L., Smith B.J., & McLean, M.E. (Eds.). (2005). *DEC recommended practices: A comprehensive guide for practical application in early intervention/ early childhood special education.* Missoula, MT: Division for Early Childhood.

Shrout, P.E., & Fleiss, J.L. (1979). Intraclass correlations: Uses in assessing rater reliability. *Psychological Bulletin, 86,* 420–428. doi:10.1037/0033-2909.86.2.420

Soukakou, E.P. (2007). *Assessment of classroom quality in inclusive preschool settings: Development and validation of a new observation measure* (Unpublished doctoral dissertation). Oxford University, England.

Soukakou, E.P. (2012). Measuring quality in inclusive preschool classrooms: Development and validation of the inclusive classroom profile. *Early Childhood Research Quarterly, 27*(3), 478–488.

Soukakou, E.P., & Sylva, K. (2010). Developing observation instruments and arriving at inter-rater reliability for a range of contexts and raters: The Early Childhood Environment Rating Scale. In G. Walford, E. Tucker, & M. Viswanathan (Eds.), *The sage handbook of measurement* (pp. 61–85). London, England: Sage.

Soukakou, E.P., Winton, P.J., West, T.A., Sideris, J.H., & Rucker, L.M. (2014). Measuring the quality of inclusive practices: Findings from the Inclusive Classroom Profile pilot. *Journal of Early Intervention, 36*(3), 223–240.

Sylva, K., Siraj-Blatchford, I., & Taggart, B. (2003). *Assessing quality in the early years: Early Childhood Environment Rating Scale: Extension (ECERS-E). Four curricular subscales.* Stoke on Trent, United Kingdom: Trentham.

Viswanathan, M. (2005). Measurement error and research design. Thousand Oaks, CA: Sage Publications.

Wolery, M., Pauca, T., Brashers, M.S., & Grant, S. (2000). *Quality of inclusive experiences measure.* Chapel Hill, NC: University of North Carolina, FPG Child Development Institute.

Zaslow, M., Tout, K., Halle, T., Whittaker, J.E., & Lavelle, B. (2010). *Toward the identification of features of effective professional development for early childhood educators: Literature review.* Washington, DC: U.S. Department of Education.

Index

Tables and figures are indicated with a *t* and *f*, respectively.